JOSHUA
AND THE CITY

JOSHUA
AND THE CITY

JOSEPH F. GIRZONE

IMAGE BOOKS

DOUBLEDAY

New York   London   Toronto   Sydney   Auckland

AN IMAGE BOOK
PUBLISHED BY DOUBLEDAY
a division of Bantam Doubleday Dell Publishing Group, Inc.
1540 Broadway, New York, New York 10036

IMAGE, DOUBLEDAY, and the portrayal of a deer drinking from a
stream are trademarks of Doubleday, a division of Bantam
Doubleday Dell Publishing Group, Inc.

Joshua and the City was originally published in hardcover in
the United States by Doubleday in 1995. The Image Books
edition is published by arrangement with Doubleday.

Book design by Claire Naylon Vaccaro
Illustrations by Kate Brennan Hall

Library of Congress Cataloging-in-Publication Data
Girzone, Joseph F.
Joshua and the city / Joseph F. Girzone.
p.   cm.
"Image books."
1. Joshua (Fictitious character)—Fiction.   2. City and town life—Fiction.
I. Title.
[PS3557.I77J645   1996]
813'.54—dc20   96-20638
CIP
ISBN 0-385-48569-7

1   3   5   7   9   10   8   6   4   2

Dedication

THIS MANUSCRIPT, of all my manuscripts the most difficult to write, and over which I prayed in tears, I very humbly dedicate to Joshua, whose ever present guidance in the lonely hours of so many nights helped me to understand the gentle, loving manner with which He passes through each of our lives, in times of joy and in times of pain and tragedy, making even the most devastating of experiences the substance of the glory that will one day be revealed in all of us who open our hearts to His goodness.

At times, writing some of the material of this manuscript was frightening, especially the section about the world of darkness. It was late at night. I was all alone. A phone call shook me. A voice from a foreign land told me of strange things happening, and of dark presences threatening. When the person hung up, I was almost afraid to continue, but the very threatening fear made me realize that what was being written had to be written, and I knew that Joshua's presence was all the assurance I needed. I still reread that passage on Satan with vivid memory, knowing how true it is. But, where there is love and God's presence, we need not fear, for no evil can touch us.

May Joshua's presence touch the lives of each one of you and grace you with his peace and joy and forever lighten your journey through this life, to the Kingdom His Father has prepared for you.

Fr. Joseph F. Girzone

JOSHUA
AND THE CITY

I

A CRISP AUTUMN breeze swept across Broadway, churning dust and debris into tiny tornadoes. The sun was bright but the air was brisk. The slim figure walking north on Broadway, dressed in khaki-colored pants and loose-fitting brown shirt, stood out in the rush of harried pedestrians. Among the thousands of varied humans wandering like ants to predetermined destinies, he seemed different. He was not hurried or harried. He emitted an aura of serenity in a sea of troubled, tense faces. He looked at people as he walked along as if to greet them. Some looked back, not noticing. A rare few smiled faintly. He continued walking on.

Passing a movie theater with flashing lights and lurid pictures, he looked, briefly noticing with no apparent reaction, and walked by. Farther on, a young girl in purple tights and pink blouse approached him. Her face, like pure alabaster radiating a youthful beauty, marred by pain and anguish, looked old far beyond the girl's tender years.

Timidly walking up to the man, she looked almost imploringly into his eyes, "Mister, you look lonely. Would you like to have a companion?" then, embarrassed at her own brazenness, lowered her eyes in shame.

"Yes, I would, very much. Would you walk with me?" he responded.

"Yes, but it will cost you. It's not for nothin', you know."

"What is your name?" the stranger asked her in such a kind voice that she felt compelled to tell him.

"Charlene," she answered. "What is your name?"

"Joshua."

"The name fits you. You look like a Joshua."

A sharp-looking, gaudily dressed dude watched the two of them from a distance. When the girl noticed him she became tense, aware she had started off badly with this her first customer, by not getting an immediate commitment from him. Joshua noticed the change in her face and realized.

"Walk with me. I will protect you," Joshua said to her.

Overwhelmed by Joshua's gentleness, the girl did as he told her.

Sensing something unusual, the dude approached the two of them.

"What's up, man? This is business. No funny work or you're dead meat."

Reaching out, he attempted to grab the girl by the arm. Joshua calmly grabbed his arm and whatever he did to him caused the pimp to grimace in intense pain; with his knees buckling, he fell to the ground motionless.

Taking the girl by the arm, Joshua walked on.

"Don't be afraid!"

"I am afraid. Not for me but for you. Don't you know who he is?"

"I know who he is. You have no need to fear. He will not remember ever having met you or me."

"Where are you taking me?" Charlene asked Joshua.

"Nowhere. You are free to walk away if you like. I can see how troubled you are and I want you to feel free to share your pain with me. I will not hurt you and I will not take you anywhere."

"Who are you? You frighten me, yet you make me feel so strangely peaceful."

"I am Joshua, and I know you, Charlene, and all about you."

Then, as he told the girl intimate details of her life that only she could know, she should have been even more frightened but felt oddly at peace.

More curious than ever, she asked him again, "Who are you?"

"At times in everyone's life, God sends someone to touch their life, to befriend them and guide their steps through dangerous paths. You asked me if I would like a companion. I knew you were the one who needed a companion. Trust me and do not be afraid. You left your home and wandered so far away. Why?"

"My life at home was miserable. My father hated me. He locked me in my room so I couldn't go out. He put a lock on the telephone so I couldn't call my friends. When he was drunk, he cursed and swore at me and called me terrible names. None of them were true. Now they are, but they weren't then. When he kicked my boyfriend out of the house one Sunday after we came back from church, that did it. I was so humiliated, so ashamed. I couldn't face my boyfriend after that. When I bumped into him by accident in school the next day, he turned and walked the other way. I was devastated. I knew then that there was no way I could live a normal life with my family. That night I packed my things and sneaked out and hitched a ride across the country."

"Are you happy now?" Joshua asked her softly and without the slightest hint of sarcasm.

"No, I guess not. But I had no money and had to earn a living. I hate what I am doing. When you're desperate, you'll do anything."

"Do you miss home?"

"I do, but I know I can't go back. I do have to grow up. I know I can't do it at home. My parents want me to be what they can feel comfortable with. I can't be myself at home. I don't know what to do."

"How old are you, Charlene?"

"Sixteen."

"Would you like to go to a nice school, if I make arrangements for you?"

"What kind of a school?"

"A good school where you can live and have all the opportunities you need to learn and grow and have fun."

"Where'bouts is it?"

"Outside the city near a small town."

"It's not one of those places for bad girls, is it?"

"No. But it is a school for girls. I know you like boys. That's understandable. It's the way God made you. And there is a boys' boarding school not far from this school. They do a lot of things together. They go to football and basketball games together. They have dances. They have people you can talk to when you are hurting. And when you are ready, you can contact your family."

"Who will pay for it if I go?"

"Don't worry about that. Have faith! God will take care of you. He loves you."

The two walked along, oblivious to everything around them. Arriving at a busy intersection, they crossed and entered a park with trees and shrubs of every description. Charlene seemed a little wary entering an isolated park with a stranger, but she sensed a goodness about him that settled her fears.

"I walk through here a lot, Joshua, when I'm hurting and feel alone. It's so peaceful. Even though I was hurt so much at home, I miss home terribly. I cry myself to sleep many times, and wish life could be happier and more beautiful than it is. See that lady sitting on that bench ahead of us! She's my friend. She's out of it most of the time. I think her husband is a rich developer. When he goes to work, she walks up here with a picnic basket and sits here staring into space most of the time. I talk to her and we have become friends. It took a while for her to trust me. She is always so frightened of strangers."

As they approached the bench, the lady looked up. Recognizing Charlene, her face lighted up and she beckoned for her to come and sit down with her.

"Jana, I'm so glad you're here today. I want you to meet my friend Joshua," Charlene said as she motioned for Joshua to greet her.

"Joshua, this is my friend Jana," she continued.

"Jana, I am very happy Charlene is your friend. I would like to be your friend too."

The woman, who was dressed elegantly and looked every inch a lady, had a frightened look as she eyed the stranger. She did not know what to make of him.

The bench was large, so Joshua and Charlene sat on either side of the woman and tried to draw her into conversation. Even though she was glad to see Charlene, she immediately retreated into her inner world and remained silent except for an occasional word to Charlene. Joshua could see she was in the beginning stages of an illness that would eventually degenerate into total retreat from reality and force her to spend the rest of her life in an institution or under constant surveillance. Watching the patience and compassion Charlene showed toward the woman, Joshua could see the young girl's goodness and care for others in spite of her own pain and misery. The woman clearly meant a lot to the girl, who was trying and hoping, perhaps against hope, that her love and kindness would bring the woman back to health.

"Jana," Joshua said to her, "have you and Charlene been friends for a long time?"

At first the woman said nothing. Then she turned and looked into Joshua's eyes to see if she could trust him. Whatever she saw reassured her and she slowly uttered, "Yes, we have been friends for a very long time," which was not exactly true, since they had known each other for only a few weeks, but the woman no longer had any sense of time or distance.

"We have picnics together," Jana continued. "I have my picnic lunch all ready. I was hoping she would come today. I miss her when she doesn't come. Since you are her friend, I will share my picnic lunch with you too."

The three of them ate and talked. Jana slowly relaxed but still had limited awareness of the world around her and every now and then retreated into the dark, empty void within her mind. When she did this, Joshua would look into Charlene's eyes and could see the pain, the pain of a desperate child who knew she was losing the only friend she had and could do nothing to hold on to her as she slipped further and further away into a world no one else could enter. Joshua saw the panic in her face, and it moved him deeply. Tears watered his eyes.

Charlene looked up and their eyes met. Like magic, a

bond developed between the two of them. Joshua just smiled, and Charlene seemed to know what he was thinking and from that moment trusted him completely. Even though she still knew nothing about him, she knew he had a soul that was sensitive and deep and that she could trust him.

When they finished lunch, Joshua stood up and made as if to leave. Charlene also stood, confused about what to do. She wondered if she was to continue on with this stranger or go back to the streets. Jana remained seated, pathetically looking from one to the other.

Joshua reached out and, placing his right hand on Jana's head, closed his eyes and silently prayed. When he finished, he caressed her face gently and, wishing her well, said goodbye. Looking at Charlene, his eyes asked her if she still wanted to walk along with him. She smiled and said goodbye to Jana.

"I hope I see you tomorrow, my dear. I miss you when you don't come by to visit me."

"I will try, Jana."

Joshua and the girl walked along the path. It was hardly a minute before a woman's voice came calling out to them, "Charlene, Joshua, wait for me."

It was Jana, leaving behind all her dignity and composure, and running up to them like a young teenager, her picnic basket slung over her arm.

The two turned, shocked to see her so full of life. When she reached them, she was happy and smiling. "Joshua, what did you do to me? When you touched me, I felt the strangest feeling coursing through my body. I felt as if a veil had been lifted from my soul. It was as if I had come back from a strange world and was alive again. Charlene, Charlene, now I can tell you how much you really mean to me. You have been my only friend in my loneliness. I love you so much. I used to think of you day and night. You were all I had to cling to as I felt myself slipping away into a dark world of fear and terror."

The two women hugged each other and cried. "You were the same to me," Charlene said through her tears. "If you only knew the fears I have as I walk the streets!"

Joshua looked at the two of them and waited for them to finish.

"Joshua," Jana continued, "thank you so very much. Charlene has become for me the child I never had. I love her with all my heart. I wish she could come home with me. I know she is all alone."

"Charlene, would you like to go home with Jana?"

"I would love to."

"I think she would have to continue her schooling," Joshua hinted.

"I know, I know. I know just the perfect place for her. My husband and I will pay all the expenses. He will be so happy when he sees I am better." Jana reached over and hugged Joshua, kissing him tenderly on his lips. His eyes sparkled with joy at seeing a dying soul come back to life.

It dawned on Charlene that Joshua somehow had known all along, ever since he met her, just what would happen as they walked along the street. Now she wondered who he really was. She walked over and threw her arms around him and hugged him with all her might, crying her heart out in a torrent of emotions.

"Joshua, Joshua, I don't know who you are, but I think you must be God or close to Him to do what you did for us. Thank you so much. I will never forget you. Never."

Jana and Charlene walked off together, holding hands along the way. Charlene took the picnic basket from Jana's arm and carried it in her free hand. Joshua watched them as they walked back toward the busy streets, then turned and continued through the park.

Emerging from the other end of the park, he walked across the street and up into a neighborhood that was so different it might have been a foreign country. Houses were dilapidated. The streets were dirty. People looked at strangers with sullen faces as if saying loudly and clearly, "What are you doing in our country? You're not welcome here."

Young men in their twenties and thirties were standing in groups along the streets, idle, glaring at him as he passed. He looked at each one and offered a friendly smile as he walked by. No response.

In the middle of the block was a fruit stand in front of a grocery store. He stopped, bought a half dozen ripe peaches, and bit into one of them as he continued on his way. Across the street a basketball game was in progress. The boys, tall and muscular, with sweat pouring down their faces, were totally engrossed in the game. And they were good. Joshua walked over and went into the yard. Leaning against the chain link fence, he watched intently.

One after another the boys made baskets, some from almost half court. No one paid much attention to the stranger, even though he was white. At one point, one of the players passed the ball too high. It bounced in Joshua's direction. Reaching out for it, he took it in one hand and aimed, shooting the ball at the basket. The boys stood motionless watching him as the ball flew over their heads.

Only their heads moved as they followed the ball more than halfway across the court. To everyone's shock, the ball dropped into the hoop without even touching the rim.

"Not bad, man!" one tall, lanky fellow shouted at him as they all went back to playing their game.

Joshua leaned back against the fence and continued to watch. Their bodies swirled and danced around one another with almost mathematical precision, hardly touching as they maneuvered toward the basket. Their playing was a work of art, not unlike a ballet. At one point, however, one of the boys tripped and turned his ankle, falling to the ground in pain. He got up and tried to continue but couldn't. Limping away from the others, he walked over to where Joshua was standing.

"Sit down and rest awhile till the pain eases," Joshua told the young fellow.

"Man," one of the boys yelled to Joshua, "do you want to take his place? We're short one."

"Yes," Joshua replied as he ran out onto the court.

For the next half hour or so they continued to play. Joshua kept up with the others but did nothing spectacular, other than making a few good shots and assisting others so they could make the baskets. He surprised everyone by passing underhanded while the others had their hands in the air, which was effective but made the boys laugh because it was so odd. Perhaps he did it for that reason.

After the game he shared his peaches with them, as they all walked up the street.

"Where do you live, man?" one of the boys asked Joshua.

"Just around," Joshua replied.

"Man, you mean you don't have no place?"

"That's right, but I don't mind. I'm happy."

"Well, my name's Gordon. This is Hakim, and this is Abdul, and this fat dude here is Floyd, and this is Karim, and this is my brother Elijah."

"My name is Joshua, and I enjoyed playing basketball with you. You are really good. You must play every day."

"There's nothin' else to do. We can't get a job any place, so we play ball. It keeps us out of trouble, and we stay in shape."

"If you don't have any place to go, you can come up to our house," Gordon offered. "We just live up the street. I'm sure Mama will invite you to stay for dinner."

Reaching the corner, the group separated. Gordon and Elijah and Joshua continued on until they reached the house, a four-story row house. The brick had long ago been painted lavender, now mostly peeled off. The wooden molding around the windows and front door, once yellow, was now brown with age and soot. The three walked up the stone stairs and entered. The hall was dark. Paint was peeling off the walls. A carpet had once covered the staircase. The outline was still there, but the wood was now well worn.

Gordon banged on the door before entering to warn his mother they had a visitor.

"Mama, we're home. Brought a friend with us," he yelled as the three walked in.

"You just come in and make yourselves at home. I'll be right with you," she hollered from the kitchen where you could smell pork frying on the stove.

Gordon led Joshua into the living room, which at one glance you could tell was well lived in. The sofa and chairs were old and, though clean, were worn out of shape. A scratched coffee table in the middle of the room was filled with magazines. A half-finished cup of tea rested on an open copy of *Ebony*.

"Gordon, you get your guest something to drink. Learn how to be a gentleman," his mother called from the kitchen.

"Okay, Josephine," he yelled back.

"And don't you call me Josephine. I am your mama, and don't you forget that."

"Okay, Mama," Gordon said, looking at Joshua, embarrassed. Joshua smiled and put him at ease.

Gordon left to get a drink for Joshua and himself. Elijah had already gone into the kitchen and attacked the refrigerator.

"What's your friend's name, son?" the mother asked as Gordon edged his way into the refrigerator.

"Joshua."

"Is he from the neighborhood?"

"How do I know, Mama? He's just a new friend. I didn't cross-examine him. He's a nice man, that's all I know; you'll like him."

As he started back into the living room, his mother followed, wiping the sweat from her brow with her apron, then drying her hands. Josephine was a pretty woman. Her face radiated her open, happy personality. She was perhaps in her early forties and still had an attractive figure in spite of four children.

Entering the living room, she held out her hand to Joshua, who stood up as she entered and shook her hand.

"Welcome to our home, Joshua. My name is Josephine, as you just heard. Are you from the neighborhood?"

"No, but I'm thinking of settling here. It is a nice neighborhood. The people are warm and friendly."

The woman looked at him, shocked. "Nice neighborhood?" she echoed, bewildered. "There are so many things going on here, it's enough to make your head spin. I'd move a thousand miles away if I could. It is no place to raise children."

"But I see a lot of goodness in the people here. They are just losing hope. That can change if people work together to make things better."

Gordon gave Joshua a glass of soda. Josephine picked up her cup of tea and sipped it. Elijah came in quietly and sat down on the arm of a chair.

"Young man, you sit down properly," his mother barked.

"Okay, Mama, okay," he said with obvious annoyance.

Elijah never said much. He had always been a thoughtful boy, inclined to be sullen at times, evidencing a deep anger that surfaced only on occasion. He was affectionate and kindhearted and would, whenever he had the means, bring home little presents for his mother. He knew she had nothing. It bothered him immensely that, as good as she was, she could never have any of the nice things other people had, particularly the white ladies who could be seen showing off their pretty clothes and jewelry down around the square. He watched Joshua intently. Joshua knew it. Although he said nothing about Gordon bringing Joshua home, Elijah struggled with the thought of his brother bringing a white dude to their house and introducing him to their mother. He knew Gordon felt drawn to this white fellow. It troubled him, especially having to cope with the thought of Joshua coming to their house often in the future. He sat on the sofa drinking his soda, saying nothing, but watching Gordon and his mother and Joshua as they conversed.

"Joshua, I like the things you say," Josephine said. "I don't know how you can like our neighborhood, though. There are so many troubles around here. I worry day and night about my children getting into trouble. I know they are good boys, but even good boys get into trouble without their even wanting to."

"I know, Josephine, but if we all make an effort things can change. Nothing is hopeless. We just have to pray and have faith and work at it. Your people are good people. They just feel they do not have a chance and it makes them desperate. But we must have hope that things will change. Each one has to do his or her share to make good things happen. Working together can accomplish wonders."

"Man, where do you start around here?" Gordon broke in. "I've been trying to get a job for months and come up with nothing. Every day I try. No one wants to hire a black man. Man, that's discouraging."

"Do you work?" Elijah asked Joshua, looking into his eyes but not able to muster the friendliness to use his name.

"I have a job to do," Joshua responded succinctly, then, turning toward Josephine, told her what a remarkable job she had done in raising her children with such good, solid values.

"Thank you. It is not easy in this kind of atmosphere. There are temptations all around for the kids today, and I pray day and night that the good Lord protect them and keep them from evil. The devil works mighty powerful in our community. The kids laugh at me when I talk like this,

18

but I know what I am talking about. And I know the Lord will not let me down."

"The Lord will never abandon you, Josephine. He will protect your boys, and your daughter as well."

"How did you know about my daughter, young man? My boys been talking?"

"No, I saw her picture on the stereo and knew it was your daughter. She looks just like you."

Tears flowed down Josephine's cheeks. "My daughter, my dear daughter, Corinne. She is such a sweet thing. She left home in the spring, to get a job and go to school, she said. She hated the neighborhood. But I don't know where she is now. I stay awake nights praying for her and worrying myself sick about her. I hope she got herself a job and a place to live. I hope she found a place to go to school. She's a bright girl, my little angel."

"Put your fears to rest," Joshua assured her. "God always hears a mother's prayers, not, perhaps, the way they like. But He always answers. Be at peace. He will protect her."

"I hope you're right, young man. I sure hope you're right."

Elijah seemed bored at all the talk and got up to leave. As he started out the door, his mother called to him, "Elijah, where are you going now?"

"Mama, I'm just going down to the corner. It's too stuffy around here."

"You keep out of trouble, young man, you hear me?"

"Mama, I hear you, I hear you. Those words pound in my brain day and night."

"We'll be eating in about half an hour. So be back on time.

"Gordon, your friend is welcome to stay for supper if he likes. We have more than enough for everybody," Josephine told her son.

"Joshua, how about it? We would love to have you. We can go out afterward and I'll show you the town."

"You are very kind. I'd like that," Joshua replied.

II

ELIJAH WAS PLEASANT during supper and even offered to go out with Gordon and Joshua afterward. The brothers took Joshua to some of their favorite haunts and introduced him to their friends. It was irregular to introduce a white person to anyone in the neighborhood, but it was totally out of order to take one into the private hangouts.

A short, fat black man cornered Gordon at the end of the bar and asked him point-blank, "What are you doing, man, bringing a white dude into our place? You know we have no room for those people here."

"He's my friend, Jake, and I want him to meet all my friends. If you like me, you like my friends, and this man is my friend. So I expect everyone to treat him the way they would treat me. And that word better get around."

Joshua was just walking through the crowd with Elijah during this exchange, so he did not hear what was said. When he and Elijah approached Gordon, Jake extended his hand graciously and introduced himself. "My name is Jake and I already know you are a friend of Gordon. Any friend of Gordon is a friend of mine."

"Thank you, Jake, my name is Joshua."

The four of them sat at a table in the corner where they could see everything going on in the room. The place was dimly lighted and filled with smoke. A band of six or seven was playing jazz at the opposite end of the room. The bar was packed tight with men and girls pressing against each other, straining to hear their voices over the din of music and loud noise. The atmosphere was oppressive, but it was home. It was neighborhood. It was community to all these people, and to them it was not oppressive. It was merely life as they knew it.

A waiter named Marco stopped by the table to take orders. Gordon introduced him to Joshua, then ordered nachos and dips for the table, and something to drink.

"Joshua, what do you think of our little hangout?" Gordon asked.

"It is good to see your brothers and sisters enjoying each other's company. You sure do know how to have fun."

"Man, that's what life's about. That's all we have left," Jake answered. "Thank God we can still have fun, or life would be unbearable."

A young lady came over to the table and sat down next to Gordon. She was an attractive girl in her twenties, with her hair done up in the tiny braids that have become the fashion among so many black girls.

"Hi, boys, you've been making yourselves rare lately. Where have you been?" she asked, sidling up to Gordon. "I've missed you, man. Thought you left town. I'm glad you came in tonight. I got some news about your sister."

Everyone perked up.

"What did you hear, girl?" Elijah stammered.

"I thought I was talking to Gordon, boy," she shot back at him as she turned back to Gordon.

"Anna Mae, this is my friend Joshua," Gordon said as the two smiled at each other.

"What did you hear?" Gordon asked her.

"I heard she's living in Queens, and with a nice family. I don't know who the people are, but they have a daughter who goes to college. Your sister goes with her and works in the cafeteria and does housecleaning on the side."

"Housecleaning?" Elijah laughed. "Where'd she learn that? She must have took a crash course."

"Anything else?" Gordon asked.

"That's all I heard, and it was a good source. At least that's good news."

"Thanks, Anna Mae. Mama will be glad to hear that."

"What's your friend do?" Anna Mae asked.

"We picked him up on the basketball court. We decided to keep him for our team. He doesn't really play the way we do, but he's real good, so we kidnapped him."

"What do you do, Joshua?" Anna Mae asked.

"I wander around meeting nice people," he answered.

"You get paid for that?"

"An unimaginable salary." He smiled.

"Don't you feel uncomfortable all alone in this wild world?" she continued.

"Not at all. You are lovable people. I haven't had such a warm welcome in all my life."

The night went fast. People were friendly to Joshua, which was a surprise, though it was obviously out of respect for Gordon, whom the whole neighborhood respected. It was only on the way home that someone confronted the three of them and tried to make trouble. There were four men walking toward Joshua and his companions. As they approached, one of them made a remark to Joshua. Gordon flared up immediately, but Joshua tugged on his arm and told him to ignore it. When the group walked past, the fellow turned and made another remark, which the three ignored. Annoyed at being ignored, the man pulled something out of his pocket to jab at Joshua, who knew what he was up to, and immediately swung around and, knocking the instrument from the fellow's hand, kicked it into the street where it dropped down the sewer. The others who were with him obviously did not want to get involved. They just ignored what had happened and walked on. Unsupported by his companions, the fellow left to catch up with the others.

Intrigued by Joshua's unusual reaction to situations, Gordon spent the rest of the way home asking Joshua questions about himself and his different way of reacting to things.

"Joshua, you know, man, you're different from most dudes I know. First thing I notice, you're not afraid of us. Here you are in the midst of a black jungle and you aren't even nervous. Second, you don't know me or my brother from nothing, yet you accept us as if you knew us all your life and are not afraid to come and stay at our house. Third, you're not arrogant. You really seem to like black folk and enjoy our company. What's with you, man, where'd you come from? And you got my brother Eddie here bewildered. I can tell. He don't like white dudes, but he don't know what to make of you. I think he almost likes you."

"Don't be wise, Gordon. And stop calling me Eddie. I don't hate white people. I just have a hard time with them. They got everything and we got nothing. Joshua seems to got nothing, too. So, I figure he can't be too bad. Like one of us, except he ain't black, but that ain't his fault."

"Getting back to where we were, Joshua, where you coming from, man?"

"I don't think I'm so different," Joshua said simply. "I

think you look upon yourself as different and expect others to think you're different. I think you are just like everyone else, though I see a playfulness and a sense of fun and a love of life in you that I don't often see in others and I just enjoy being with people like that. I don't see you as different."

"Those four fellows that passed us back there, we could have taken them on easily and wiped them out. Why did you avoid them?"

"Gordon, why stoop to their level? If they have a problem, why get involved so you end up with their problem? You may demolish them, but is that any reason to feel proud? Dogs in the street do that and we look down on them as animals. Why become an animal? There are more intelligent ways to conquer an opponent. One of them is to win him over to your side. If you beat him, he becomes your enemy and one day you will meet him again, when he is stronger and a greater threat than ever. Win him over, and you have a friend. That takes discipline and intelligence. Any animal can fight. It takes intelligence and goodness to win over an enemy. He will never again be a threat to you. Isn't that a better way to win a fight?"

"Guess I can't argue with that," Gordon answered. Elijah just listened.

At the house, Josephine was still waiting up. As old as the boys were, she still couldn't get herself to go to bed until they were home safe.

"Mama, you still up," Elijah whined. "We'll be old men and you'll still be waitin' up for us. We're old enough to take care of ourselves."

"I was just watching the TV, son. It helps me relax before I go to bed."

"Mama, say what you want, but we know you stay up because you worry about us. We don't get into trouble, so why are you always worrying?"

Josephine said nothing, just walked to the kitchen and turned on the pot of coffee that was all ready to brew. While it brewed, she brought into the living room a plate of cookies she had baked while the boys were out, then got the coffee and served it.

"Mama, we got some good news about Corinne down at the club," Elijah blurted out.

"What did you hear?"

"Anna Mae told Gordon."

Josephine looked at Gordon. "What did she say?" the mother asked excitedly.

"She said Corinne is staying with a friend and her family across the river. The two of them go to college together, and Corinne does housecleaning to earn money. Anna Mae didn't tell me who told her, but she said her source was very reliable, Mama, so you can put your heart at rest."

"Why doesn't she call or contact us? She must know how much I worry."

"Maybe she did contact you through Anna Mae," Gordon interjected. "Perhaps she's trying to break loose, so she can be independent. You know it's not easy being independent, Mama. No offense but you are a very strong woman, and you always know what's good for us. Corinne is just like you, Mama, and she has a pretty good idea of what's good for her, too. Just be happy she's doing good. I know her. She'll get in touch when she feels secure enough in her freedom."

"Well, boys, I'm turning in. Don't you stay up late. You need your sleep too."

With that she left for her room. The others retired shortly afterward. Joshua insisted on sleeping on the sofa in the living room.

III

JOSHUA LEFT AFTER breakfast the next morning. The two brothers asked if they could go with him. The three walked off, down past the basketball court and into the park. Josephine felt an unusual serenity in her sons' newfound friendship and breathed a silent prayer as they walked out the door. Even though this new friend of her sons did not appear to be one of their kind, and even though he was really a stranger, there was something authentically good and wholesome about him that made her proud that her sons wanted to be close to him. All the values and ideals she had tried so hard to instill in them seemed to finally be taking hold, so the quiet prayer of thanks.

When Jana's husband came home from work the night before, he was so stunned to see his wife in the kitchen cooking, he hardly noticed the young girl helping her.

"Jana, my dear, what happened to you? You're like your old self. And roast pork! Like old times; it smells delicious."

"Oh, Dan," she said as she turned to kiss her husband, "the most wonderful things happened today! I don't know how to tell you. I don't even know where to start," she blurted out in such a rapid burst of excitement, her husband could hardly keep up with her.

Then, noticing Charlene, Daniel asked, "Who is your visitor, Jana? I don't remember meeting her before."

"Oh, this is Charlene, the friend I have been telling you

about, the one I have lunch with in the park," she responded as she introduced Charlene to her Dan.

"Why don't we all sit down and relax for a few minutes while we are waiting for the roast to finish," Jana said excitedly, "and I will tell you everything that happened today."

"Will you have a drink, dear?" Daniel asked as he prepared a drink for himself.

"No, thank you," she answered.

"Charlene, how about yourself?"

"No, thank you, Mr. Trumbull. I don't drink. Maybe a glass of hot water and a lemon, if it's no trouble."

"Hot water and lemon? That's an interesting twist," he responded with a grin.

"Yes, I got attached to it as a kid and I still like it. I really do enjoy it."

"I'll have to try it myself sometime, when nobody's watching," Daniel said half in jest.

Jana told the story of her daily visits to the park and how she and Charlene had become such good friends, and how much she used to looked forward to Charlene visiting with her each day. "Dan, I knew something was going wrong inside, but I did not know what it was. I could sense I was losing contact. Our friends stopped calling me and I was getting so depressed. You were so kind and understanding, dear, and tried to keep me from feeling insecure and inadequate, but I knew something terrible was happening, and I could do nothing about it. Charlene was the only friend I had.

"Then today, the oddest thing happened," Jana continued as she told her husband about Joshua and how he and Charlene came walking into the park together and sat

34

down with her and how they all had lunch, and that before he left, Joshua put his hand on her head and just closed his eyes, and how she felt the strangest feeling of warmth course throughout her body and knew something had happened to her. "It wasn't until after Joshua and Charlene left and were walking down the path that I realized I was healed and was whole again."

Dan wanted to believe but was skeptical. Charlene could see it and reassured him that what Jana said was exactly what happened. She also shared her own encounter with Joshua before their walking through the park. Her honesty in telling Dan about how she met Joshua impressed him and piqued his interest. Now he was curious to meet this unusual fellow who would pick up a prostitute on the street and just take a walk with her.

"Jana, I would really like to meet this man," Dan said seriously. "Whatever he did for you, I have to admit, I'll be forever grateful to him, and for bringing you back to me whole. Do you think he will be in the park tomorrow?"

"I don't know," Charlene said. "I don't know if we will ever see him again. I had never seen him before."

"Nor have I," Jana added.

"Do you think you and Charlene could take a walk up to the park tomorrow to see if he is there? Perhaps you could invite him to the house for dinner, say next Sunday."

That night after everyone had gone to bed and Dan and Jana were alone, she told Dan about Charlene, all about her: her difficult family life, her running away from home, how the two of them had become such good friends as they met each day in the park, how Charlene befriended her when all her other friends drifted away as her sickness became noticeable.

"Dan, I would like so much for her to stay with us. She has no one, and she cannot go back home. It may seem sort of strange, but it was almost as if Joshua had given the two of us to each other."

"What do you mean, dear?" Dan asked, as he reached out to put his arm under Jana's head, so she could snuggle up to him.

"Well, the way he watched Charlene and me. I could tell he could see how much we meant to each other and how desperately Charlene needed a friend. He asked Charlene if she wanted to go with me. It was almost as if he felt responsible for her, and yet he had met her only a few minutes before. It was as if he had known both of us all our lives and understood our pain and how we needed each other."

"But, Jana, we hardly know this girl. Do you know what it would be like? It would be like adopting her. That's a frightening responsibility. We don't know whether we could trust her. We really don't know anything about her. I'm afraid."

"I can understand. Can she stay with us so we can get to know her better? I think you will find that she is a very nice girl."

"We at least owe her that. After all, she is your friend and she looked out for you when you needed someone. And she never asked you for anything?"

"Never once, not even for a penny. And I'm sure she had nothing. I think once you meet Joshua you will feel more comfortable about Charlene," Jana said in an attempt to put Dan's mind at rest.

"Well, I always did want to have a child. Looks like we're going to end up with a fully grown one," Dan said resignedly as if he sensed how things would turn out. "And she does appear to be a good girl, unusually well mannered."

"Dan, I do love you. Thank you so much for putting up with me when I was out of it. I was so afraid you would get tired of me."

"Darling, my love for you was always total. No matter what happens, I will always be faithful to you. You are mine and that's that. I know you would be the same with me. Our love has always been special, since the first day we met. Now let's get some rest. I have a big meeting with the mayor and the zoning people tomorrow, and I want to be wide awake."

"Good night, dear!"

"I love you, Jana. Good night."

Gordon and Elijah asked Joshua a thousand questions about himself as they walked through the park. Elijah's questions were heavy and cynical, like "What's your agenda, man? Why are you hanging around our neighborhood?"

Joshua did not take offense. He knew the boy was troubled and was patient with him.

"Very simple, Elijah. I like what I see here and I want to bring my Father's love into your neighborhood."

"Who's your father, man?"

"Our Father, God."

"You mean Allah?"

"Allah, Yahweh, God, same person, different languages," Joshua replied calmly.

"You don't think Allah's love is in our community?" Elijah continued.

"I've seen God's love in your mother. She is a godly woman. I saw God's love in the girl, Anna Mae, in the club last night. I did not see God's love as we walked through the streets yesterday and last night. I saw resentment and hatred in people who really don't love God. They use Allah as a rallying cry to hatred of their neighbors. That is not God's love. Those kinds of people find a morbid joy in blaming their misery on others, rather than admitting that they are what they have chosen to become. I have come to show the way out of that misery and to heal wounds. People must realize there is one God, not two who are enemies of each other, leaders of opposing armies. There is one God Who created one family whose members must love and help one another."

"You come on like you're going to make us all over, man. You are one strange dude. You speak like you are one of us. Are you one of us? Are you white or are you black? You confuse me. You sometimes look like you're white, then sometimes you look like you're black, then sometimes you look like both. I can't figure you out nohow."

"Does it really make a difference?" Joshua asked patiently. "Why can't you just accept me as I am? My parents and I at one time lived in Africa. Then we moved to other places. Like you, I am a child of our Father in heaven. Does it make a difference what part of the sun we live under? Can a finger on the right hand say to the finger on the left hand, 'Who are you? I don't know you, you are a stranger, so I will not work with you'? We are all part of the same family and we all must help one another."

"Joshua, ignore him," Gordon interrupted. "He just ignorant, man. He don't know what he says half the time. Brother, why do you have to talk like that? This man is our friend. Why can't you accept him as a friend and treat him like a friend? I don't understand you, Eddie." Gordon was clearly exasperated with his younger brother.

"Gordon, let him be! I understand your brother," Joshua said. "Let him say what is on his mind. It is good to talk about it. When something is troubling you, it is better to talk about it than to keep it locked inside smoldering where it can one day explode and do harm."

"I like you, Joshua. You know me better than my own brother," Elijah said. "I know I am angry. I can't help it. I'm just angry. I don't know why. I just am. I don't like being angry. I get up in the morning and I'm already angry. How do you stop being angry when you wake up in the morning already angry?"

Joshua could not help smiling at the almost comic sincerity of the young man, who did not like being what he saw in himself. Comedians are fundamentally serious people. The comical mask is merely a cover for their pain. Elijah had the makings of a good comedian. He even had a face that made one want to laugh, although he was seething beneath the surface.

"Elijah, you are very sensitive," Joshua said. "You have a kind heart and you like to see people happy. The pain and injustice you see around you among innocent people make you sad and angry. These things are not easy to deal with. God is not pleased with them either. He could destroy all the mean and unjust people in one stroke if He wanted to, but He doesn't. He has to respect the free will He gave people. But He also realizes that this is not the only world. This world is only a world of shadows reminding us of the real world where God lives. Knowing this, He is patient and makes other plans, and in these plans the wrongs are righted, and those who are victims become the privileged ones and are specially blessed by my Father. He puts up with a lot in this world because He knows it is for only a short time. Those who hurt and are deprived here, He makes it up to them a thousandfold in His own world, where they will have unimaginable happiness, while the greedy and the unjust will stand by begging for forgiveness, hoping they will receive even a token share of the others' good things. Be patient! God knows what is happening. He just bides His time. We have to adopt His viewpoint if we are to keep our sanity and balance. Learning to develop God's patience also helps. Do not let anger possess you. It will eat away at your very life and eventually destroy you."

As the three walked through the park, they approached the area where Joshua and Charlene had met Jana. Jana and Charlene were sitting there.

When they saw Joshua and the others coming down the path, even though they were expecting him, they seemed surprised. Joshua noticed them and smiled as they drew closer, though he did not seem particularly surprised.

"Joshua!" Jana said with high-pitched excitement in her voice. "We've been waiting here for almost an hour hoping you'd come by. We didn't know if we would ever see you again."

Joshua introduced his new friends to the women as they gathered in a circle and talked. Jana told Joshua how happy her husband was when he came home the night before and saw her back to her old self and cooking supper. "He wants so much to meet you, and wants to have you over to our home for dinner Sunday afternoon. Can you come?"

"Yes, I can, and I will enjoy meeting him," Joshua told her.

"He already likes Charlene very much, and I am sure she will become part of our family," Jana assured Joshua, sensing that he may have in some way known about Daniel's reservations about keeping Charlene permanently.

"We eat around five o'clock. Can we expect you about four, if that is convenient?" Jana asked.

"That will be fine," Joshua assured her.

Jana and Charlene left and wandered back toward the avenue. Joshua and his companions continued on.

While Joshua and Elijah were talking along the way, Gordon just listened, with a multitude of concerns churning in his mind. One of them was his difficulty in finding work. It bothered him. It continually ate away at his self-image that he was a young man, and felt useless and without value, a drain on his family because he was not productive. It was not that he did not want to work. He got part-time jobs here and there, but they did not last. When he was laid off he felt worse than ever. It was just another rejection.

"Joshua," Gordon said, "how do you keep so peaceful? You seem so much like us, but you don't seem to have hangups."

"Peace comes from attitudes, and from striving for goals you set for yourself," he replied. "I have my goals. I work toward them each day. I know in my heart I am accomplishing my Father's will, so I am at peace and I am happy. It is really simple."

"I guess I don't have any goals. It is hard to set goals when you have no means to attain them," Gordon responded.

"Everyone should have goals, dreams that fire the engine of our ambitions. Goals are a sign of hope, a sign that we are alive and haven't given up."

"But you have to have a job to afford your goals," Gordon added.

"Only if your goals are material. You can have a number of goals. The overriding goal of your life should be to please your Father in heaven and to work at perfecting yourself. Other goals are finding a place of honor among your neighbors and accomplishing good things so your passing through this world will enrich the lives of others."

"That's one big task, man," Elijah protested. "How would you know even where to begin?"

"You begin by taking responsibility for your life. No one else is responsible for who you are or where you are at. Take pride in knowing you are a child of your heavenly Father. That bestows on you a great dignity. Then decide to live worthy of that calling. The kind of work you do does not matter. Every kind of honest work is noble. Every individual has talent of one kind of other. Develop that talent. Earn a living by it."

"But where do you start and how do you start?" Gordon asked.

"What kind of work would you like to do?" Joshua asked him.

"I would like to make things."

"Well, that's a good start. You could make things for people in your neighborhood. You might start out by learning to repair and upholster furniture."

"Where can we learn?" Elijah asked him.

"I will show you if you like."

"You know how to do it?"

"Yes."

"Where do we get the furniture?"

"Maybe your mother would like to have some of her furniture fixed. Ask her."

"That's not a bad idea. Then, if it looks good, maybe our friends will let us fix theirs if we don't charge too much."

"That's right, and then you will have started your own business."

The young men could not wait to get started. On the way back home they stopped to play basketball with some of their friends, then went home for supper. Joshua was becoming a familiar face in the neighborhood.

IV

FINDING A SUPPLY store for tools and material was a problem. These were necessary if Joshua was to teach the brothers their new trade. It took them half the day just to locate the places that sold what they wanted. Finally they managed to acquire everything they needed to get started. The furniture was in such bad condition, getting Josephine's permission to experiment on it was the least of the problems. Picking the fabric had excited her, and she just hoped they would do a good job of renewing the sofa. It was special.

"If you do a good job with my sofa, I'll let you work on all the other pieces too. Are you sure you know how to do this kind of work, Joshua?"

"Yes, I do, Josephine, so don't you go worrying yourself. You will be delighted with your boys' workmanship when they are all finished."

They did not get a chance to do much the first day. Most of the time was taken up tracking down what they needed to do the job. The next day, however, they started work in earnest, tearing the sofa completely apart down to its frame. Josephine could not imagine her boys ever putting the thing back together again in any shape that could be considered presentable. Unable to watch any longer, she decided to take a walk, a long walk so she at least did not have to watch. Maybe they would surprise her, but her hopes for that were not very high.

The three of them worked hard all day, not even

stopping for lunch. Gordon and Elijah were shocked at Joshua's deftness in knowing just what to do.

"Man, you are good at this. What's your line of work anyway?" Elijah asked him, mystified at his know-how.

"Creating," was Joshua's simple answer.

"Creating? Creating what?" Elijah continued.

"Everything."

Not realizing the full import of Joshua's answer, Elijah let it go at that. By noontime they had replaced the springs and had refastened and reglued some of the loose pieces, so the frame was tight and fully secured. The springs were sturdy. Everything was ready for the fabric to be attached, which took a good part of the afternoon. They were hoping they could have the whole job done by the time Josephine returned. They had two of the three pillows finished when she walked up the stairs. Hearing her come, they cut her off at the door and told her not to go into the living room.

"Mama, you just go into the kitchen and fix the supper. We will be all finished by the time supper is ready," Gordon told her.

It was hard for her not to look. That sofa had been a wedding present from her father. It meant a lot to her because of all the memories attached. She was afraid to even think of what it must look like, but she went along with their enthusiasm just to show her support and confidence in them.

The trio worked feverishly so they could surprise her and have it all finished by the time supper was ready. Joshua had accurately calculated the amount of material needed to stuff the pillows.

"I hope you are all finished in there because this supper isn't going to wait for no one," Josephine yelled into the living room.

"Just one more minute, Mama, and we are going to give you the surprise of your life," Elijah yelled back excitedly.

"You sure do sound excited about it. I hope your work matches your excitement, because I sure don't want no disappointment."

"Okay, Mama," Gordon called out to her. "You can come in now," he said as they pushed the sofa against the wall and picked up all the junk and tools off the floor.

Elijah ran out to the kitchen so he could bring his mother into the living room blindfolded, with his hands over her eyes. Leading her into the living room, he stationed her across the room from the sofa, then took his hands away from her eyes.

"Okay, Mama, you can look now."

The woman was wide-eyed with disbelief. Thinking she was going to witness a mess, she stood there mesmerized, and speechless. What she saw was a brand-new sofa. Only the wooden frame was old. The sofa was new and it was beautiful.

"Boys, I can't believe it, I can't believe my eyes. It is absolutely beautiful. It is even more beautiful than the one Papa gave me for my wedding. It is a work of art."

"No, Mama, a work of Joshua," Elijah interjected with pride not only in bringing home such a good friend but in himself and his brother in having learned a trade in such a short time, and having learned it so well. They were justifiably proud of themselves. Only Josephine was more proud of what they had all done, and in so short a time. She could finally see some hope for her sons.

Walking over to Joshua, she threw her arms around him and kissed him with a love and gratitude she had never so freely given to anyone before. Tears rolled down her cheeks in torrents.

"Joshua—" She started to say something, but her crying made it impossible to understand. Joshua just hugged her and let her rest her head on his shoulder. The boys shifted from one foot to another, embarrassed at their mother's sudden show of such emotion. She always appeared so tough with them on the surface, though they knew she had a soft heart. This was one of the rare times she showed it.

"Well, let's eat supper. You sure earned it tonight."

"But you still owe us for the sofa, Mama," Elijah reminded her.

"We'll take a little off for the supper," Gordon added.

What happened would probably be a little thing in most people's lives, but for that family it was a major event, opening the door as it did to a future now bright with hope.

All they talked about at supper was the sofa and how perfectly professional it was. Gordon praised Joshua's ability with great pride, remarking that after all that was his job, creating. At which Joshua just smiled. The simplicity of these people was touching. It was the same simplicity Jesus talked about in the gospels. To see it in real life was a pleasant surprise.

After supper the boys could not wait to get on the phone and call all their relatives, asking them if they needed any furniture upholstered. Asking who would do the work, they all laughed when Elijah told them he and his brother would do it.

"But we're really good," Elijah told them. "Come over and see the job we did on Mama's sofa. And we'll do just as good a job on yours."

Josephine ended up reassuring everybody that they really

would do a good job, and they would be reasonable, too. She would make sure of that.

Seeing Josephine's new sofa was a good excuse to get together and socialize, so in no time the apartment was filled with aunts and uncles and cousins. Everyone did like the sofa, so the boys got a string of orders. Joshua enjoyed watching the boys' enthusiasm as they showed off the sofa and explained the workmanship that was involved.

Some of the relatives took Joshua for a relative. Surprisingly, his dark sunburned complexion and Mideast features did show similarities to their family traits.

"I am happy you think I'm part of your family," Joshua said. "You have a remarkable family. I am amazed at how you care for one another."

During the night Gordon approached Joshua and showed him all the orders they had, and all the different kinds of furniture. "Do you think we are going to be able to do all this kind of stuff?"

"Don't worry about it! The work you did on the sofa is the most complicated. That is an old-fashioned piece of furniture and was difficult to work on. Whatever you do now will be easy."

"Will you be around to help us?" he continued.

"Yes. Don't be afraid! Have confidence in yourself! You now know you can do it. All you need is the practice until it becomes routine. I'll stay for a while to show you other things you need to know and also how to take care of books. You're going to have to keep records and pay your taxes. When you make money, you have to share and help others. That's the way families work. Be conscientious about that!"

For the next two weeks Joshua helped the brothers with their work, showing them how to repair difficult or complicated pieces of furniture. The customers were extremely happy with the brothers' workmanship and were even happier with the prices they charged. Word spread about their work and new orders came in each day. Joshua did not stay around all during that time, but just as they needed him. Having made friends with the brothers' relatives and friends, he wandered through the neighborhood familiarizing himself with life in the community.

When the time arrived for his dinner date at Jana and Daniel's, he arrived at the building just before four o'clock. As the doorman was not to be seen, Joshua walked into the foyer and wandered around looking at the flowers and the sculptures that adorned the magnificent entrance. He could see the doorman talking on the telephone so he waited. When the man finished, he was surprised to see this plainly dressed stranger wandering around the foyer. Since Joshua was so commonly dressed in his khaki pants and casual shirt and sandals, the man thought he was a vagrant and peremptorily asked him to leave. When Joshua tried to say something the man would not give him the chance and forcibly ushered him out the door, telling him to keep away from the place or he would call the police next time.

At about that time the phone rang. The doorman closed the door behind Joshua and went back to answer the phone. It was Daniel Trumbull. It had occurred to him from what Jana had told him that Joshua would probably not be well dressed and the doorman might need to be prepared for his arrival.

"Thank you, Mr. Trumbull, I shall receive him with all due respect when he arrives and send him up to your penthouse immediately."

Horrified, the man ran to the front door and, going outside, tried to find Joshua. Fortunately, he was standing on the corner watching the pigeons.

"Mr. Joshua, Mr. Joshua," the frightened doorman called out to him, "I have made a horrible mistake. I thought you were one of those vagrants who wander the streets all day. I did not realize you were a guest of Mr. Trumbull."

"There is no difference. Whatever you do to the least of my brethren you do to me," was Joshua's simple reply.

"Yes, I know, I know. I am terribly sorry. I beg you please not to tell Mr. Trumbull what happened. I am awfully ashamed."

"Don't worry about it. It is just between the two of us. But remember, you never know when God is coming to visit you. He usually comes dressed like the poor."

Joshua still arrived upstairs promptly at four o'clock. They were all delighted to see him and gave him a warm welcome.

"Joshua, this is my husband Daniel. He's been a blessing to me, staying with me during my illness. I have told him all about you."

The two men shook hands, genuinely happy to meet each other. They all proceeded to the living room, a spacious room looking out across the vast park with its extensive woods and trails. The room had windows on all three sides, making possible views of the sun on its rising and setting and the vast area in between. The Trumbulls were extremely wealthy, having each inherited fortunes from their families and having used them to acquire extensive real estate holdings and make wise investments to build what they already had into a vast financial empire. They were, however, among the few truly wealthy persons who not only realized that wealth does not bring happiness, but who also had the goodness of heart to be sensitive to the masses of people around them who had nothing, and not just build monuments to their own memories. Joshua's meeting Jana in the park was not by chance, but a response to the pain of two good people whose own hearts generously responded to the pain and heartaches of others.

Daniel had been curious to meet Joshua. His wife, and Charlene too, had talked of nothing else all week, and had portrayed Joshua in the most glowing terms. Daniel listened with not a little skepticism. He was impressed, nonetheless, and realized there had to be something unusual about Joshua. He had met all kinds of people in his work and was impressed with how far the human spectrum could stretch, and how strangely different people could be, for better or for worse. He knew Joshua had to be somewhere way out on that spectrum. He was hoping he was not going to be disappointed.

It was not far into their conversation before Daniel realized that Joshua *was* different, far different, from anyone he had met. What struck him most was that, as heroic as this man appeared to be, there was a balance in his manner and in his thinking and in his vision of reality. His words manifested an encyclopedic intelligence capable of comprehending the most difficult circumstances, no matter how complex, and a clarity that cut through all the nonsense of life and saw reality stark naked. Along with this was the rare ability to express his thoughts with such simplicity that even a child could understand. As highly intelligent as he was, Daniel was impressed with his rare common sense.

Commenting on the grand city spread out before their eyes, Joshua made the remark that "as magnificent as this city is, it is bankrupt and on the verge of collapse because it does not appreciate the vast genius and potential of its poor, and treats them as irrelevant to life and an unwanted problem. Developing the genius of the poor is the secret to the resurrection of this community."

That remark impressed Daniel and stuck with him the rest of the evening. He kept bringing it up to Joshua, wanting to discuss it in fuller detail, wondering what was in his mind when he said it. He sensed there was a world of experiences churning in Joshua's memory for him to express his judgment in such a sharply concise statement. It was not just a chance remark made on the spur of the moment to stimulate conversation. He began to feel a kinship with Joshua.

Joshua knew Daniel and what he said was carefully calculated to stimulate Daniel's thinking on matters which were of critical importance. Joshua had his plans and many things would happen before the evening was over.

Realizing that the ladies were just listening and being left in the background, Joshua asked Charlene how she liked her new home.

"Joshua, I never dreamed I would be living in a palace like this. I'm almost afraid I'm going to wake up and realize it is just a dream and find myself out on the street again."

"Stop thinking like that, Charlene. You are very special to us," Daniel said. "I can now see that your meeting Joshua and Jana was not an accident. I can see it was only too carefully planned by Someone outside ourselves. I believe we are all a gift to one another. I want you to feel that this is your home and we are your family. So stop worrying about finding yourself out on the street again. There is no way my little girl is going to be out on the street."

Jana was beside herself hearing Daniel say what he did. She could tell her husband liked Charlene, but he had been reluctant to commit himself to keeping her, and Jana did not know whether he would be willing to make a commitment to accept her as part of the family. She rose from the sofa and went over and kissed her husband. "Darling, I can't thank you enough. I was praying all week you would love her. I know she will bring happiness to us all."

Daniel turned beet red. He was very reserved in public and rarely showed emotion. This outburst flustered him. He looked at Joshua. They both smiled. They were a lot alike and Joshua understood his feelings.

The supper was pleasant. The conversation was light. Everyone was getting to know each other, so no one wanted to talk seriously. It was their first dinner together. There would be many more, and there would be occasion enough to talk about serious matters.

Before Joshua left, however, Daniel did take him aside in his den and have a brief personal conversation with him.

"Joshua, I don't know what you did for my wife, but she is completely herself again for the first time in months. I will be forever grateful to you for your kindness to a person who was a total stranger. I want to show my gratitude to you but am at a loss as to what I can do. I see you are not a worldly person, so money has no meaning to you. You must have some dream that is important to you. If you would share it with me, perhaps I can help you to fulfill that dream."

"Daniel," Joshua replied, "you have no need to thank me. What I did I did because I wanted to. You and your wife are good people with deep faith. My Father rewarded that faith. You have no need to repay me."

"I appreciate your feeling that way, but I still want to do something. I would be honored if you would allow me."

"I know you have vast wealth. God has blessed you with riches. Look out the window there. You see those blocks and blocks of poor people. They have no hope. They have no future. Give them a future."

"Joshua, how can I give them a future?" Daniel questioned, a little disappointed at Joshua's request.

"I know it may sound impossible. But I will help you. Buy up those blocks and tear down the buildings and rebuild that whole section of the city. Employ the people who live there to do the work. Give them jobs. In doing that you will give them dignity and pride. We can work on the plans together and design it in such a way that the new neighborhood will be self-sustaining, a place where people can not only live but also work. New schools can be built for the children where their talents can be developed and they can be prepared for jobs and learn to feel a sense of personal worth. Many of those children are geniuses but are not college material. Their genius dies in their breasts because no one cares. The anger, the crime, the drugs, are expressions of their frustration. Locking them in prisons is not the answer. They need to be given hope. The neglect of political leaders and business leaders in not aiding them to lead productive lives is just as criminal as the behavior of the young people in the streets. If you don't imprison the one, why imprison the other? Prison is not a solution. It is the government's admission of failure to solve a problem. After a person's release from prison, the same environment still exists, and still demands a solution. That solution is development of young people's talents and the providing of jobs for them so they can develop a sense of pride in themselves. That can be done without sending the kids to prison."

"Joshua," Daniel said with a smile, "that is quite a dream. I am not going to say no, because I did ask you what you would like me to do for you. But if you are willing to share your vision with me so I can better understand how such a project could be workable, I will be only too happy to work with you. I can buy up all the property, and I can tear down all the buildings, but what do we do with the people, and how do we rebuild in a way that will make the living situation any better than it is now?"

"I do have a plan, and it *is* practical, and it *is* workable. I will share it with you in detail if we can spend some time together during the week."

"Joshua, that's a deal," Daniel said. "But if we decide it is not practical or feasible, I hope you will allow me another option to repay your kindness. How about lunch this coming Tuesday?"

"That would work out fine. You are a good man, Daniel, as well as a shrewd businessman."

The two men retired to the living room and spent a while longer talking, then Joshua got up to leave.

"Joshua," Daniel said, "I hope I am not being rude. But we would be honored if you could spend the evening with us. As you can see, there is plenty of room. There are only three of us and there are five bedrooms. I realize you haven't brought anything with you, but we have everything you need right here."

Joshua did not need much encouragement. The night was a little too chilly to spend in the park, which is where he would have gone.

V

BREAKFAST THE NEXT morning was brief as Daniel had
to be at his office for appointments. He and Joshua left
together and parted at the entrance. When the doorman
noticed the two of them emerging from the elevator he was
embarrassed and, though he was properly polite to Mr.
Trumbull, he could hardly look at Joshua. He just hoped
that Joshua had not told Mr. Trumbull about how badly he
had treated him the day before.

When the two men parted, Joshua went back uptown to
see how the brothers were doing with their new business.
The boys were not home but their mother gave him the
address of where they were working and called to see if they
were still there. It happened to be one of Josephine's
relatives. They were still there and would be glad to have
Joshua come over to give them a hand. They were having a
difficult time sewing leather. They had not expected to do
anything in leather.

When Joshua arrived, the two brothers were trying hard
to keep calm. "Man, I never thought I'd be so glad to see
you," Elijah said, perspiration rolling down his face.

"What's the matter, Elijah? You look like you're ready to
tear everything apart," Joshua said.

"I am. Gordon and I have been working on this thing
for two hours and can't get the damn thing straight. We
already wasted two good pieces of leather. You didn't tell us
we'd have to work with this stuff, man."

Joshua laughed. Elijah fumed.

Gordon was sitting there watching his brother. Elijah was too impatient and Gordon found that it was better to leave him alone when he got that way. Hearing that Joshua was coming to help convinced him it was better to wait until he came and showed them how to do it.

"Well, what you have done so far is excellent," Joshua assured them. "A little uneven in a few places, but not noticeable. Leather is not as easy to work with as fabric."

"Tell me about it," Elijah broke in exasperated.

"It is unforgiving, and not as pliable," Joshua continued. "Also you need stronger needles and a tougher thread. Your sewing machine is strong enough. You could invest in another one, a more professional model, when you have saved some money. But we can finish this job with what we have. However, we will need stronger thread to work on what you are doing now. So don't do any more until we get it."

Joshua asked Elijah if he would go and get the thread. While they were waiting, he helped Gordon cut out pieces for the remaining sections of the sofa. When Elijah returned they were ready. From that point on things went smoothly and, though they finished later than planned, they got the job done to the customers' satisfaction and were even paid before they left.

"This working for relatives is bad business," Elijah muttered. "They expect you to work for nothing. And we got so many relatives, we'll be working for nothing for the rest of our lives. We got to get some good-paying customers if we're going to enjoy this work."

Joshua just laughed. "Look at all the practice you're getting. Strangers would not be as easy on you as your relatives."

He knew they still made good money from the jobs, so did not feel sorry for them. Gordon was happy and told Joshua their business was booming even with the discounts for family. They were proud of the fact that they had made over five hundred dollars profit on the three jobs they had done since they last saw Joshua. And they still had ten more lined up.

When they finished they went back to their house. Josephine was delighted to see Joshua.

"Joshua, what a nice surprise!" she exclaimed on seeing him come in with her two boys. "Those two have been working hard at their new job. They sure do like the money. They never had so much money in all their lives. And the nicest thing about it, Joshua, is that they are having fun doing it."

"I'm sure they will use the money wisely," Joshua responded.

"They are. They already sent some to their sister. I am sure she can use it. She's a good girl. Can you stay for supper?"

"Yes, I would be more than happy to. This is the best private restaurant in town."

"Thank you, friend. I consider that a rare compliment. I know you have excellent taste."

Supper was brief as Josephine had to go out immediately afterward. The boys took Joshua to a club to hear some jazz and meet some friends. Joshua slept over that night and left early the next morning.

The streets were quiet in the early morning. There was hardly a person in sight. Walking through the neighborhood, he passed the many empty, burned-out buildings and boarded-up store fronts. As dilapidated as the surroundings were, the air was still fresh, as street traffic was light.

Approaching a church, he noticed a group of women and a few men standing in front talking quietly. He stopped to chat with them. They were friendly and told him they were waiting for Mass to start. "Where are you from, young man?" one lady asked him.

"Just visiting friends and taking my early morning stroll."

"Aren't you the gentleman who's been teaching my nephews how to fix furniture?" a man asked him.

"Yes, they are very industrious fellows. They'll have a good business someday."

"Well, I appreciate what you do for them. My name is Jerome Dixon, and I am mighty pleased to meet you. I know your name is Joshua. I can't tell you what an honor it is to have this chance to talk to you. These are my friends," he said as he introduced them all to Joshua. "We come to Mass in the morning when we can make it. If you would like to come with us, we get together afterward downstairs and have coffee and doughnuts and socialize and have Bible and a little prayer time. You will be more than welcome. I'm sure the others will be happy to meet you."

"Thank you. I appreciate that."

They walked up the steps and into the church. Joshua sat a few pews behind the others. About fifty or sixty people were sprinkled throughout the old vaulted building, mostly women, but a few men among them. There was a handful of white folk as well, people from another generation who had lived there all their lives and were not going to leave though their children had long since married and moved away.

These black folk were now their neighbors and they were all good friends.

The priest who offered the Mass was black, a jolly teddy bear of a man. His vestments were like robes African tribesmen would wear, of many bright colors. Three people, a young lady about twenty and two men a little older, were sitting in the sanctuary with the priest. One man was lightly tapping on a tall drum, creating an eerie mystical mood as the ceremony was about to begin. The girl had a small reed instrument in her hands. The other man was holding an odd-looking wooden instrument. The people began to chant softly, not the kind of music one would ordinarily hear in church, but strains of a music you would expect to hear in Africa. It was quiet music and peaceful and strangely prayerful. The priest greeted the congregation and invited them to sing along with the musicians.

"My friends, we gather here in the quiet of the morning to offer our worship to our Father in heaven, to thank Him for all the good things He has so generously bestowed upon us, even for our pain and our hurt, and to ask His help and protection during these most difficult times.

"We also ask Him to be merciful to us and forgive us all our sins, and give us the grace to live in a way more worthy of our calling as His children."

The other two musicians then began to play. The music was soothing, and spiritual. It lifted one's soul into an atmosphere of peace and serenity which made communion with God flow easily. The priest chanted quietly, calling down upon his people the blessings of God as they gathered early in the morning to praise Him and ask His help and healing for themselves and their loved ones.

The lectors who did the readings read first in English from the Old Testament, then from the New Testament, then read the same lessons in an African dialect for the benefit of a few newcomers to the neighborhood. There were people from Africa who had recently settled in the community, enough of them to adapt the liturgy to accommodate their needs. The priest spoke of the importance of people not adopting the values of the world around them, but by their shining example bringing the love and light of Jesus into the empty lives of many of their neighbors.

"We do indeed live in troubled times but do not lose hope, no, no, never lose hope. The good Lord will one day come to save us from the troubles that surround us. We must believe this. He will not abandon us. We must pray unceasingly for Jesus to again come and save us from the terror that surrounds us on all sides. We know He will come. We know He will hear our prayers. We must not lose hope. The Lord Jesus is always near to save us, if only we are willing to trust and open our hearts to receive Him."

After Mass most of the people went downstairs to socialize for a few minutes. As some had to go to work they did not stay long. Some who had nothing to do afterward stayed for quite a while. The priest came down for a few minutes, was introduced to Joshua, made a few comments to the group, then left. Joshua mixed in well after Josephine's relative introduced him. His affability and humor won their hearts.

"Now you make sure, young man, that you come again. We like you already and we want you to feel at home here," a lady in her forties said to Joshua as they were well into their socializing.

"I sure do feel at home," Joshua responded to her. "You

people are very special. Everybody should be as warm and accepting as you are."

After about an hour the group broke up, picking up the dishes and washing them, then walking out together.

Joshua continued his walk. A lady asked if she could walk with Joshua, as she would like to talk to him.

"By all means, Georgeanne," Joshua said, remembering the name when they were introduced.

"Mr. Joshua," the woman began, "I watched you out of the corner of my eye during Mass. You were completely absorbed all during the Mass. I have never seen anyone pray so intently. You must be very close to God. I knew I just had to talk to you. Do you mind?"

"Not at all. I am glad."

"I am beside myself. Living in this neighborhood is like living in hell. The pressure on the young people is frightening. Sometimes it's too much for them. One of my sons. He's a good boy but he's so weak. I know he takes drugs. He denies it. But I know. He started out on marijuana, but I know he's taking something a lot worse. His personality has changed. He is so different from what he used to be. I can tell his mind is obsessed with the stuff, and he can't focus for long on anything else. I know there is nothing I can do, but I just can't stand by and watch him destroy himself. He's got a girl down the street who goes to those spiritual meetings where they have séances and contact spirits and dead relatives. She's been trying to get my son to go with her. I am so afraid. I think they are involved in devil worship. I stay awake half the night worrying and praying for my son. I go to Mass for him every morning, but I don't see any change. I don't know whether God is even listening to me. Maybe I'm not good enough for God to hear my prayers. I know I wasn't a model of virtue when I was young, but I have told God so many times how sorry I am for the past. Do you think God will help my son even though I am so unworthy?"

"Georgeanne, stop worrying, stop beating yourself. Remember the words of Jesus: 'Look at the birds of the air. They do not sow nor do they reap, nor do they gather into barns. Your heavenly Father takes care of them. You are worth more than all the birds of the air.' So stop worrying. Your heavenly Father knows your pain and your torment. He also watches over your son. He loves him too. Your son has much to learn yet. He is still unwilling to give up the pleasures of life and his curiosity is a trap to him. And even though my Father has helped him so many times, he still clings to his attachments and is slow to learn. Your prayers have been instrumental in keeping him from events that could have destroyed him, but God listened to your prayers and protected him. If you knew the things that could have happened to your son and did not, you would realize how close God has been to him all this time. He will continue to help him, but he may have to go through a frightening ordeal if he does not learn soon. Continue praying. Your prayers will in the end be answered. Trust me, and you will see. A mother gives birth to her children not just once but twice. The first time physically, the second time spiritually. The spiritual birth is just as painful. Do not worry. That is my Father's job, to be concerned. You just pray and know that He will answer your prayer. My Father loves your son more than you ever could. And He watches over him every moment of the day and night."

"I can't help worrying. I am so afraid."

"Worrying is natural. But, as your trust deepens, the

worrying will diminish. It is important that you have peace. You have your life to live with all its concerns. That's plenty for one person. Just pray; it is much more effective than worrying. Believe me! My Father listens and He cares."

"I don't know why, but I do believe you. I know you are close to God. I will try not to worry. I do feel better already. I hope it continues."

"Be at peace, it will."

"Could you please talk to my son sometime? Hopefully you might be able to touch his heart. He is not a bad boy, just confused."

"I would be happy to, Georgeanne."

"We live only a few blocks from here. We are all home most of the day or not too far from the house. So whenever you come we will be there. Just go down the street there two blocks, turn left, and we are the third house down, number 411."

"Be at peace and trust in my Father's care."

The woman thanked him and left. Joshua continued his walk. The neighborhood was coming alive as people were starting out on their way to work. Homeless people were scattered here and there, lying on cardboard, resting their heads on bags containing the sum total of their worldly possessions. Joshua tried to talk to some of them, but they were uncommunicative, so he walked on. The sun was now higher in the sky and its warm rays soaked everything in sight, coaxing the sleepy world to wake up to a new day and a new life. Joshua basked in its warmth. Its penetrating rays soothed and caressed him, filling him with the joy of being alive.

Walking across town, he approached a riverbank, where he met a man fishing. An oil tanker floated lazily, effortlessly upriver. Deck hands waved to the two figures on shore. Joshua and the fisherman waved back.

"Catch anything?" Joshua asked casually.

"Not a damn thing. And I've been out here for half the night, it seems."

Joshua smiled, remembering those same words and practically the same conversation so many, many years ago.

"Try a little farther out and just a bit upriver. I think you'll do well," Joshua advised.

The man took Joshua's advice just to be congenial and was shocked to hook a fish almost immediately. Then another the second try, and a half dozen more after that.

"Man, you're a walking sonar. You should come down here every morning, and I wouldn't have to waste so much time catching my family's supper."

"This is your supper?"

"Yes, sir, since I got laid off it's been mighty difficult making ends meet. At least, since we all like fish, we can save money by my coming down here every morning. This great catch will give me a couple of days off. I'm grateful to you for your help, but I still don't know how you knew those fish were there."

"Sonar is as good as anything, I suppose," Joshua answered as the man walked off with his gear and pail of fish.

"If you ever come across a place where they need a good machinist, I'll be right down here by the river," the man yelled back as he left. "And my name is Walter."

"Mine is Joshua. I'll see you again, Walter."

VI

STANDING ON THE bank, surveying the surroundings and admiring the view, Joshua pictured to himself the many possibilities of the site for neighborhood gatherings. The saucerlike setting was a natural amphitheater, deep enough to accommodate a large audience, yet shallow enough to allow audience participation in events if occasion arose. The site would need some cleaning up, but that would be relatively easy. This was the type of setting Joshua liked. It was practical for many reasons.

With a smile on his face, he walked away from the river and started back into the neighborhood. The streets were busy now with people and heavy traffic. The fresh, clean air of early morning had given way to pungent, noxious fumes from car and truck exhausts.

Joshua walked down through the park and into the subway where he took a train to Daniel Trumbull's office for their noonday meeting. Daniel was glad to see Joshua and asked if he could wait for a few moments until he was free, then they could leave for lunch and spend some quiet time without being bothered by interruptions.

"Do you have any preference for food, Joshua?" Daniel asked as they walked from the office to the elevator.

"Not really. My best friends were fishermen, so fish was always available," he replied.

"There's a nice seafood restaurant nearby, and there is an excellent Thai restaurant."

"Why don't we try the Thai restaurant?" Joshua said. "That sounds like it might be exciting."

"Their food is different, but it is tasty. I think you will like it. The atmosphere there is quiet and we won't be disturbed or have to rush. We can just sit and talk and you can share all your ideas with me. I have to admit, you are a fascinating man, and I look forward to getting to know you better. This lunch should give us a chance to get better acquainted."

"Thank you. I am glad you are willing to take the time. I know you are very busy. I have been thinking over what we talked about the other night, and I have more details to share with you, which will make the plan seem more realistic."

"Good. I have some ideas as well which I would like to discuss with you."

The lunch turned out to be a three-hour brainstorming between the two men. Joshua had a comprehensive, detailed plan for the whole neighborhood north and west of the park and over to the river.

"The country needs a model, Daniel, and you are the one who can do it," Joshua told him. "The cities are too crowded, and industry as it is in big cities cannot absorb so many people."

"What do you propose?" Daniel asked.

"That whole neighborhood north and west of the park is old and many of the buildings are dilapidated and rat-infested. There are so many people in the area and no place for them to work. Why not tear down the buildings and plan a whole new concept? You could have clusters of one- or two-family houses, and a few apartment buildings sprinkled throughout the area with a limited number of apartments.

There could be a park in each little neighborhood where children could play so they wouldn't have to play in the streets. I can picture building mini-factories and machine shops scattered throughout the area, with national corporations setting up operations to provide work for people in the neighborhood. New schools would have to be built but a different kind of school, funded by industry and administered by a locally elected school board composed of representatives from the business community and local residents. Children would take courses based upon their abilities, many of them apprenticeship courses preparing the students for work in the local factories or laboratories or offices. Students who are college-oriented would take the courses they need to prepare them for college. Industry could also provide some of the teachers for the more technical courses. An essential requirement for all teachers would be that they love children and love teaching."

Daniel sat there listening intently, trying to digest everything Joshua was saying. "Joshua, you realize that is a revolutionary concept for a city like this. I don't know whether we could get cooperation from all the people we would need to agree to a plan of this magnitude."

"I realize it may be different, Daniel, but it is practical for a city like this and it is the only way you can give hope to the people who live here. There is so much crime here because people have no hope. They are not born evil. They become desperate because of circumstances. Society pays them to stay poor and lazy and destroys their initiative and sense of pride. This plan will give them a chance to develop dignity. You could build all kinds of little businesses in the area, with stores owned and operated by neighborhood people. Funds could be made available for local people, to prepare them to operate their own small businesses. I know it will be difficult in the beginning because few of the people have experience in business, but with patience many of them can be successful. There are plenty of shrewd people who fail at business. Poor people deserve a chance even if some do fail.

"Community centers and recreation centers could also be a help to building up morale. And, an important factor, when construction begins most of the work could be done by people who are already living here. They should be the ones to demolish the old neighborhood and rebuild the community. It would give them all a deep sense of personal pride that they built everything with their own hands."

"Joshua, you sure are a dreamer!" Daniel said as he finished his last bite of dessert.

"But you have to admit, it is practical and realistic. And it will work."

"I can see it can work all right. I can also see a thousand obstacles to putting it all into play."

"But then, Daniel, since when did you let obstacles discourage you from the vast projects you have been dreaming up for years?"

"You are right. I never was one to let obstacles get in my way. But I don't know how much revenue this kind of a project will generate."

Ignoring the last remark, Joshua added one last item to his dream. "And can't you picture a park on the river where there could be dances and concerts and all kinds of programs in the summertime? With imagination, there are unlimited possibilities. Remember, Daniel, when we die, God is not going to ask us how much money we made but how much we gave away and how we used the gifts and abilities He gave us to help others."

"I know, my friend. I could have done a lot more. I do have to admit that this could be a wonderful accomplishment. Perhaps it could inspire others to duplicate the idea in other cities, and even in other parts of this city. Joshua, let me think about it and talk it over with my advisers—not that they are going to decide, but they can come up with all the negatives. If I can knock down their major objections, then I think we might be able to do something. I do like the idea. I admire you, Joshua. For a simple man you sure do think big, a lot bigger than even I would have dreamed.

"Now, I have some concerns to share with you. You will have to be patient with me. I am not as verbal as you, and my thoughts don't come as easily."

"You were patient with me. I can do no less."

"I am so deeply touched over what you did for my wife and over Charlene's solicitude for her. It prompted a lot of thinking about those kids on the streets. As I was walking to a show the other night, I bumped into a whole string of them along the street. Some of them looked tough, but many of them seemed like innocent kids. It must have taken a lot of pain to force them to live like that. I can't imagine it is by choice, with all that can happen to them. They have no life now and they certainly have no future. I know I can't adopt them all, and the Covenant Houses can do only so much with them. I was thinking perhaps I could get a group of businessmen and women together and set up a program to send many of those kids to school. I am sure some of them are bright and would do well at a boarding school. Others we could send to good private day schools and build residences for them to live in, or place them in apartments. What do you think?"

"I think it is an excellent idea. Those children have been deeply wounded, most of them. Some of them may have just been stubborn or obstinate and they are going to have to work out their problems on their own, because they will give headaches to whoever tries to help them, but many of the children could really benefit from someone caring for them. I think your idea will work. You might want to talk to the people at the Covenant Houses and others like them. They would be able to screen for you those who would benefit from a program like that. You also might want to provide jobs for them so they can develop a feeling that they are helping themselves. It is important for their sense of personal pride. You are a good man, Daniel. I am glad we are friends. We will accomplish much together."

"Yes, with your brains and my money, I can see how we can go far, if I don't go broke. Why don't we get together again, say, Sunday night for supper at my place?"

"I will look forward to that. My peace will go with you, and your family, till then."

"Joshua, you know you are welcome to stay at my house at any time."

"I know that, Daniel. Thank you."

The two men parted.

Joshua walked along the avenues and streets, admiring the sights and looking in store windows, intrigued by the endless inventions of the human imagination to entice people to part with their money. In big cities like this, one could always manage to encounter funny characters on street corners, like the walking peanut, or Mickey Mouse, or a clown of some sort. Joshua bought a bag of apricots and ate them as he walked up the street, sharing some with a homeless lady he encountered on the way. She was at first wary, then thanked him and took what he offered her.

As the afternoon wore on, it began to drizzle. Joshua worked his way back uptown and decided to accept Daniel's invitation to stay at his house for the evening as the weather was turning bad.

VII

JOSHUA ROSE EARLY and prepared breakfast for the others. His presence was always special as it carried with it a sense of peace and serenity. When they finished eating, Joshua left and went up into the park where he spent part of the morning talking to people he met along the way. It was unusual to see a stranger striking up a conversation with people he had never seen before, but Joshua's manner was so personal and unaffected that it disarmed people and made them feel immediately at ease. He had a rare insight into each one's life and gave each person an awareness of how special they were to God, and how important was the message their lives preached to so many others they encountered each day. Coming from anyone else, such talk might have seemed trite. Coming from Joshua, it had an air of authority about it that deeply affected the listeners. Each one walked away touched and very thoughtful.

As he left the park he continued up into the neighborhood and walked to the street where Georgeanne and her family lived. Arriving at the door, he looked for a bell. There was none. It was a three-family house, so he knocked at the door until someone opened it.

"Does Georgeanne live here?"

"Upstairs, mister," a little girl answered.

"Thank you."

Walking up the stairs, he knocked at the door. Georgeanne opened the door and was shocked to see Joshua standing there.

"Joshua, come in, come in. I have to admit, I am surprised. Did you have any trouble finding our place?"

"No, not at all."

Ushering Joshua into the living room, she motioned for him to be seated. She sat down across from him. As school was still in session, the younger children were not at home. Only Jeremy, one of the older children, was there in the process of getting dressed. He had just finished shaving and was drying his face with a towel.

"Jeremy," Georgeanne called to her son, "this is Joshua, the nice gentleman I have been telling you about. Come over here and say hello to him."

Embarrassed, the young man walked over with the towel in his hand, still wiping his face, and held out his other hand to greet Joshua. "It's nice to meet you, Joshua. My mother thinks you're the greatest, man. She don't think that about too many men, believe me."

"Thank you, Jeremy," Joshua responded. "You're quite a young man yourself. Your mother must be very proud of you," he said with conviction.

"I'd feel a lot better about myself if I had a job. I feel like I'm a real drag on the family."

"Your value is in what you are. A job does not give a person value, as necessary as it is to survive. Don't worry, you will find work soon. Take it seriously and work hard. You will get ahead. Help your family when you're successful."

"Thanks, sir. I wish I could be as confident as you are."

"Jeremy," Georgeanne broke in, "would you bring in a cup of coffee for Joshua and myself, and for yourself, too, if you are finished shaving, and then come and sit down with us."

After heating the coffee, Jeremy brought it into the living room and served it. Joshua watched him and saw the good that was inside the young man. He could see why his mother was so concerned for him.

"Thanks, Jeremy," Joshua said as he served him the coffee.

"You're welcome, sir," Jeremy replied.

"Joshua, Jeremy is the boy I was telling you about the other day."

"Mother, you embarrass me."

"Son, I know what you are going through. It is not easy to go through it alone. It is a very rare honor for us to have the good fortune to have someone as good as Joshua to help us. I know all your dreams, son, and I know how easy it is to destroy all our dreams, living in this neighborhood. We have to be so strong and have such deep faith and be so close to God just to survive. I know that Joshua can help us. We may not have many more chances, Jeremy, and I know that, deep down, you want to get past all this pain and hurt."

Jeremy said nothing, just looked very pensive.

"Would you tell Joshua, son, about some of the things that take place at Jennie's 'family circle'?"

"Mother!"

"Jeremy, don't be afraid. Joshua understands. Tell him, so he can share with us what he thinks."

"Mother, I only went once, and I was afraid. It is strange. They all sit around on the floor. The room is dark. The leader tells everyone to be quiet, very quiet, and just to let their minds rest and relax and be open to the other world. After a while things happen. The leader tells you things about family you never dreamed anyone even knew about. And they are true. He also talks about loved ones who have died and delivers messages to people in the circle from deceased loved ones. And tells them things only the family could possibly know about. He also tells them that they should not be afraid of death, because after death everyone is going to live a good life and will go through various stages of development after death. There is no need to be afraid of hell because there is no such a place, he tells the group. Everyone feels good after the meeting. He also encourages everyone to be kind to one another. I really don't see anything wrong with what they do, Mother. It is all very positive."

"Joshua, what do you think?" Georgeanne asked him.

"Jeremy, Jennie also uses a Ouija board, doesn't she?" Joshua said to him.

"Yes, how did you know?" Jeremy asked.

"I just know, Jeremy. Tell your mother what happened last week when Jennie and you were using the Ouija board."

"Oh, we were just playing with it. Well, we had the thing on our laps. We were asking the thing questions. The first question we asked was: 'Is anyone guiding the movement of the indicator?' After a real long time the indicator started to move. It finally landed on the letters Y-E-S. Then we asked it: 'Who?' The indicator moved again and settled on the letters S-A-T-A-N. Then we asked it a third question: 'Who is your worst enemy?' And the answer came very clearly G-O-D. But it is only a game."

"Jeremy, do you think a piece of cardboard and a piece of wood can give answers to questions?"

"No."

"Do you think God would play games with people?"

"I guess not."

"Jeremy, the devil uses those things to entice people into communicating with him and seducing them into thinking he is their friend by satisfying their curiosity. Before you know it you are addicted to needing him for answers and, like drugs, you will do anything to satisfy that need."

"But it seems so innocent. At the meetings the people are encouraged to be good to one another."

"Jeremy, Satan was the brightest of the angels. When he was in heaven his mind was as sharp as a laser. He could not imagine anyone being greater than he, and in his pride found it very difficult to show honor to God. Now he uses his keen intelligence to seduce good people. To do this he has to make himself appear good and his intentions to appear to help people. His schemes are shrewder than any human mind can fathom. Only God's grace can help a simple human to understand the trickery of Satan and avoid his snares. Without God's help the human mind is no match. Satan is very clever in the way he leads souls on the path to hell and an eternity of loneliness with people who have never learned to love and are totally self-centered. Imagine an eternity of depression. Satan cannot tell people he is leading them to such an end, so he makes them feel very nice all the way there by telling them all kinds of things they like to hear."

"Joshua, it is hard to believe. They all seem so nice," Jeremy said.

"They have to appear nice. If they were not nice they would attract no one."

"Where does Jennie go on Sunday afternoon?" Joshua asked him.

"I don't know. She wouldn't tell me. She said they have

a meeting with some friends. She told me the street it is on and roughly where it is, but didn't tell me the exact address."

"I would like you and your mother to come with me to that place on Sunday."

"But I really don't know where it is."

"We will find it. Do you love Jennie, Jeremy?"

"Yes, sir, very much."

"We have to help her. And if you really love her, you have to be strong, very strong. Drugs sap your strength and stunt your ability to grow and face life in a mature way. They weaken a person's mind and will and lead right to Satan's doorstep."

Jeremy lowered his eyes. He knew Joshua knew he was taking drugs and felt ashamed. He wanted to fight them but was having a difficult time. It was not easy to fight them by oneself. He loved Jennie deeply but even his love for her was not enough to fight this insidious addiction. He sensed the terrible trap he was in and was frightened especially at learning that the devil could be such a real factor in his and Jennie's lives. Georgeanne looked at him and felt helpless to do anything. It was like watching someone you loved drown and you were helpless to do anything about it.

"Joshua, if Satan encourages people at these meetings to do good, and to live good lives, what is so wrong about that?" Jeremy asked.

"That is the way he starts, Jeremy, but what he does in time is to switch the focus of people's love and loyalty away from God to himself. Once people are loyal to him and committed to him, then they will follow him anywhere. By that time they will have lost any attachment they may have had to God or to Jesus. Faith in God evaporates, true holiness becomes distasteful, and love of spiritual things turns sour. From that point on the people are well on their way to eternal perdition."

"Joshua, we will go with you on Sunday," Georgeanne said. "Jeremy, what time do the rituals start, do you know?"

"I think around eleven o'clock in the morning."

"I'll be here on Sunday morning," Joshua told them. "Jeremy, this is not going to be easy, but if you pray hard and are not easy on yourself, my Father will give you the strength to overcome this affliction."

Joshua got up to leave and as he did so he put his hand on Jeremy's head. Jeremy was still sitting in the chair in deep thought.

"Thank you so much for coming over, Joshua," Georgeanne said as she accompanied him to the door. Jeremy followed and told him he appreciated what he was trying to do. When Joshua left, Jeremy broke down and cried uncontrollably. His mother knew how much he was hurting. But the crying was good. It was cleansing. "Help me! Help me, Mother, I am so afraid!" She hugged him and held him tightly, as she had when he was a little boy waking from a nightmare.

VIII

THE SUBJECT OF Satan and the occult has always aroused curiosity. Even people who profess not to believe in the devil are still curious when the subject comes up. The spirit world is beyond our ken and when anyone professes to have some experience of the beyond it cannot but arouse our interest. With so many people writing about their own out-of-body, near-death experiences, our eagerness to learn more about the phenomenon is intensified. Even doctors and others with a scientific background have of late become interested and are writing books about the subject. Everyone is curious about the origin of these experiences: what causes them, are they objective experiences of the world beyond, is God trying to stimulate our faith in the reality of life after death, are they tricks of the devil to convince us that we need not fear death because everyone is going to have a good experience after death, so Jesus' redemption is irrelevant, and we do not really need Him?

While some may exaggerate or overdramatize the work of Satan in the everyday Christian experience, there are things that happen whose timing and chain of related events are so clearly connected that one cannot but conclude that they are more than mere coincidences, and seem to point to the involvement of forces from beyond our visible material world. Jesus made the remark one day that "Satan goes about seeking whom he may devour." Scholars may interpret those words in various ways, some contending that Jesus never even said them, but the gospel quotes Jesus as having said them and, until proven otherwise, they can be considered to be the words of Jesus. One thing is certain, Jesus' knowledge of the other world is beyond question. He tried so often to warn His followers of Satan's wiles that His words should be taken seriously. Satan would like to remain anonymous, of course. He cannot afford to be exposed or to be viewed as evil. So, while he is plotting the destruction of humanity, he often does this work under the guise of good, often of freeing people from those who would limit and restrict human freedom. "If you eat of the tree of good and evil you will not die, for God knows that on the day you eat thereof, your eyes will be opened and you shall be as God, knowing good and evil." The agents he uses to accomplish his evil plots have to appear to be good and concerned only for the good of humanity, while they go about poisoning people's minds, tearing asunder sacred relationships, sowing dissension among people who have heretofore been friendly, and undermining spiritual values that have guided the world for centuries. The almost universal breakdown of morality throughout the world is not just coincidence. There are explainable causes of many of the evils we see today, but there are also many frightening things that seem to be beyond our control and even beyond our understanding. What causes a three-year-old child to kill an infant, or a young man to stab a young girl to death, then drink her blood? We do not know what causes these bizarre tragedies. We may never know. But it might be well to consider Jesus' advice to be on our guard against the evil forces that surround us.

The Sunday following the meeting at Georgeanne's house, Joshua arrived as he had promised. In fact he was precisely on time for breakfast. The family had just returned from church and were in relatively happy spirits.

"Joshua, your timing is perfect. We just sat down for breakfast," Georgeanne said as she opened the door. "Come right in and make yourself at home."

Jeremy stood up as Joshua walked in and shook his hand. He was glad to see him and showed it.

"Peace to everyone," Joshua said as he came in and sat down at the kitchen table. All the children were present, and were curious to meet Joshua.

"Joshua," Georgeanne said as she introduced her children, "this is my family: Esther, Judith, Nathan, and you know Jeremy."

"You are a good mother, Georgeanne, and you have a remarkable family. You should be proud."

"I am, but we do have our problems sometimes."

Georgeanne asked Judith, the youngest, to say grace.

"Dear God, thank you for this food and for giving us a mommy who is the best cook in the world. Bless us all and help us to love one another, and bless Joshua too. And please let him help Jeremy."

Georgeanne looked at Joshua out of the corner of her eye. He smiled at the child's simplicity. Jeremy winced, then broke into a smile. The food smelled delicious, but it disappeared faster than the mother could put it on the table. It was everyone's Sunday favorite: grits, sausage and eggs, and jam.

At ten-thirty Georgeanne, Jeremy, and Joshua got ready to leave. "Nathan, you be good to your sisters now while we're gone. We'll be back in a little while."

"Can we go out, Mommy?" Esther asked.

"No, we won't be long. You stay here and play inside until we get back. I don't want you out on the street when I'm not around. And be nice to one another."

Walking up the street, the three were quiet. Jeremy was thoughtful. Georgeanne had so many things on her mind, it was hard for her to even make small talk. Even Joshua was pensive as if gathering strength for the confrontation he knew was imminent.

"Joshua," Jeremy said, breaking the silence, "aren't you afraid of what we might run into?"

"No, son, the enemy cannot hurt us if we are close to God. It is only when souls are deserted places deprived of love and divorced from God that Satan has power over them. People should not presume, however, to battle Satan by themselves. That is dangerous and can lead to the most frightening consequences. But I know Satan, and my Father is always by my side, so what I do I do not do on my own."

"This next corner, we turn left," Jeremy told Joshua.

Crossing the street, the three walked down the block. Georgeanne was becoming visibly nervous.

"I think it is one of these houses, but I don't know which one," Jeremy said.

Suddenly, Joshua began to gag and to heave violently as if he were going to vomit. His face became beet red. "This is the place," he said. "The stench betrays the presence of the Evil One."

"Joshua, are you all right?" Georgeanne asked.

"Yes, I am all right. The devil's presence is always offensive to those who know him."

"I don't smell anything," Jeremy said.

"Neither do I," added Georgeanne.

"I know when Satan is nearby. The air is always foul and oppressive. That is how I knew we would find the house," Joshua told them.

Walking up the stairs, they approached the door. Jeremy and his mother hesitated.

"Do not be afraid!" Joshua reassured them. "Nothing will happen to you. Trust me!"

Joshua opened the door and walked into the empty hallway.

Further inside the house, a group of spirit devotees were gathered around a table. On the table in the middle of the living room were a chalice and bread, mimicking the Eucharistic meal. Dressed like a priest, the leader was lifting the chalice. As he did so, a look of terror crossed his face. Immediately slamming the chalice on the table, he shrieked in an unearthly high pitch, "There is a presence here! Who let him in? Who let him in?"

The others, who had been resting on pillows on the floor, sat up and looked around, agitated. They were confused and frightened. Some stood up, wrenching their hands and sweating profusely. "What is happening? What is happening?" they said in unison, as if the people themselves were not speaking, but a chorus of strange voices speaking from within each of them.

Joshua opened the door and walked in. Something had come over him. He no longer looked like the casual free spirit walking the streets; an aura of majesty surrounded him, and a powerful sense of authority radiated from his person. The leader shrieked in agony and, with his face contorted in a terrifying expression, yelled at Joshua, "What do you want from us, Son of God? Why have you come to torment us? We know you, we know who you are. You are the Holy One of God."

The people in the circle picked up the chorus, "We know you, we know who you are, Holy One of God."

"You are Jesus, the Son of God," the leader continued.

"The Son of God, the Son of God," the others said almost in a chant. It was unnerving. Jeremy and Georgeanne stood there transfixed by what they saw, paralyzed with fear.

"Who are you?" Joshua demanded.

With frightened looks each one answered, starting with the leader. "We are many," he said in absolute obedience to Joshua's command as if in terror of his presence. "I am Mahkai."

The others followed suit: "Sura, Tooma, Makee, Bondo, Macumba, Yamuga," and on and on. It was clear they were not the names of the people in the room. It was just as clear the voices were not theirs. The accents were from strange languages totally foreign to anything identifiable.

As Joshua raised his hand they all cowered. "Do not send us back, Son of God! Do not send us back to that horrible place! Have pity on us and let us wander the earth!"

Speaking in a voice of commanding authority, Joshua ordered them, "Leave these people, I order you, Mahkai, and all your cohort. Leave these people and do not harm them. I order you to depart far from here and leave these people in peace."

Immediately the spirits left them. A look of serenity replaced the terror and agony that bound them. Totally exhausted, they fell to the floor. Looking up at Joshua, not realizing all that had happened, they saw the powerful love that radiated from him like a charge from an infinite source of energy. It filled their beings with a serenity and a strength they had never before experienced.

Jeremy had been watching Jennie and the transformation that had come over her. He walked to her and held her close to him as she hugged him and put her head on his shoulder and cried uncontrollably.

"You now know the evil that prowls the world," Joshua said to them. "Your drugs and your lives empty of love seduced you into this. If you do not want worse things to happen, you must learn to love your families, and your neighbors around you, and let the love of God fill your hearts. You cannot go through life concerned only about yourselves. You must learn to care for others. It is self-centeredness that draws Satan to your empty, troubled souls. Leave here in peace and heal the wounds of those who love you."

As they left they gently stroked Joshua's arm, as if to say thank you. Some asked if they could follow him wherever he went. Those who he could see were weak he told to follow him. The others he told to take God's love into the lives of their neighbors.

The leader, with a scowl, walked silently past Joshua, not daring to look at him, afraid even to be in the room with him. Though Mahkai had left him, he was obviously still clinging to the spirits and was frightened of Joshua. Joshua knew he would be trouble again, an individual so filled with venom that only hell would seem to satisfy such hatred.

Joshua turned and walked out with Georgeanne, Jeremy, Jennie, and the five who were to follow him.

"Georgeanne, you are a strong woman and I know you have a family already. But do you think you can help me and be a mother to these young people?"

"Joshua, how can I say no to you, when I have seen and witnessed so much this morning? I feel honored you have been so kind as to come and visit us. I will care for these children as if they were my own. I know some of them and their families. I know they are troubled. I would be happy to love them."

The five persons belonged to neighborhood families. James was the oldest, being twenty-three. His sister Carrie was seventeen. The others, two boys, Jonah and Andy, and a girl, Vicki, were all in their mid-teens.

As they walked down the street together Joshua talked to them, telling them how important it was for them to love themselves, to love what God had placed in them. They might not be perfect, but the bad image they had of themselves was not healthy. God knew they had faults and made mistakes. His Father never intended to make them perfect but gave each of them just what they needed to do a special kind of work for Him. As for the rest of their personalities, there were glaring imperfections, but that was all right. They would in time grow to be what God wanted them to be, but only in God's good time. In the meantime, it was important for them to know that God loved them just as they were. If God loved them, then they had all the reason they needed to love themselves as they were, as God made them. That was critical to their survival. They must also learn to break out of the shell of self they had built around themselves and start thinking of others. Concentrating on self is depressive and destructive. Concern for others is redemptive and healing.

Georgeanne took everyone to her house afterward, where she served them breakfast, which none of the five had eaten. While she was preparing the food, Joshua talked to the others in the living room. Georgeanne gave her own children permission to go outside and play. By midafternoon, the five young people left. A short time later Joshua left and went to visit Josephine's family.

Josephine and her boys were glad to see him, the boys particularly as they were impatient to share with him the dramatic success of their business venture.

"Joshua, you will never guess what happened," Elijah said, all excited.

"Tell me."

"We got a phone call a few days ago from a government agency. They have a huge office full of furniture they want us to reupholster. We have to bid on it, and if you help us, with your shrewd business head, we'll surely get the contract. Will you help us?"

Gordon just listened. He was happy to see his younger brother happy and thinking positively for a change.

"Yes, I'd be glad to help you," Joshua replied. "Give me all the details tomorrow and together we will work up the bid. How is the rest of your business?"

"Good," Gordon answered. "We've been getting orders from people other than relatives, Lord be praised. We put over twenty-three hundred dollars in the bank this past week. Man, that's not chicken feed. We've finally got a business, a real business."

"Don't you boys forget your poor mama when you come

into your kingdom," Josephine said, chuckling. "Maybe one of these days I'll be able to live like a lady and not have to work every day, then come home and work half the night here."

"Mama, we're not going to forget you. How we ever going to forget you with all you've done for us?" Elijah said. "And we're not going to forget our sister either. We'll make sure she gets a good education."

"I know you are good boys. I don't have to worry," she said in reply.

Josephine invited Joshua to stay for supper, but this time he declined, and left a short time later to keep his engagement with the Trumbulls.

IX

THE ATTITUDE OF the doorman at the Trumbulls' was much different this time. He could not have been more gracious. You would think Joshua owned the building, the man was so deferential. Joshua, of course, was his usual self and acted as if nothing had happened.

"Good afternoon, Mr. Joshua. It is a pleasure to see you again. The Trumbulls are expecting you, sir. I hope you have a pleasant evening."

"Thank you, Simon. I am looking forward to seeing them. They are such good people."

"That they are, sir. That they are. And kindly give them my regards."

"I'll do that."

When Joshua rang the doorbell, Daniel answered. "Well, look who's here!" he said, acting surprised.

Jana walked out to see and was so excited. She wasn't expecting him, as Daniel had said nothing about Joshua's coming so he could surprise his wife and Charlene. And they were surprised.

"Joshua! How nice! Charlene, guess who's here to see you?" Jana cried out.

"It could only be one person. I'm not exactly the number one socialite in town." She came out into the foyer and ran into Joshua's arms. "Joshua, how I've missed you!" she said, crying tears of joy.

Daniel stood there grinning, giving himself away.

"You knew all along he was coming tonight," Jana said.

"That was why you didn't want to go out this evening and suggested I cook extra food. How could you do such a thing? And we are not even dressed up!"

Daniel laughed, knowing they were so happy to see Joshua that they could not possibly be angry.

"Joshua, come in," Jana said. "I was wondering if we were ever going to see you again." Holding his hand, she led him into the living room.

"Well, you will have to tell me all about your meeting with Daniel during the week. I know you two met, but since he never tells me anything, I'll have to find out from you. I hope you had a productive lunch. I know Daniel enjoyed himself. He was so filled when he got home, he didn't even eat supper, which was a first. Here, sit down and make yourself comfortable while I take the roast out of the oven. Charlene, will you mash these potatoes? No, never mind. Why don't you just sit there at Joshua's feet like Mary and I'll play Martha. I know you want to be with him. You won't get much time later, once we all start talking."

"Thanks, Jana! You're an angel."

Joshua sat on the sofa. Charlene sat down on the floor and rested her arm on the sofa as she looked up at him. He looked at her and smiled. "Charlene, you look so peaceful. Are you feeling better?"

"Yes, I feel a thousand times better than I did, thanks to you. I help Jana during the day. She has so many things to do. I didn't realize what an important person she is. She has an office and secretaries and is involved in a thousand things around the city. Even the governor called her the other day to talk to her. It must have been a terrible thing for her and Daniel when she got sick. They are both such loving people with all their wealth and power. Joshua, I can't thank you enough for what you have done for all of us. It's like a miracle."

"Charlene, always remember, when you are hurting, it is only for a while. My Father watches over you constantly so no evil will touch you and no harm will come to you. So don't ever be afraid. My Father will always protect you and watch out for your good."

While Joshua and Charlene talked, Daniel helped his wife in the kitchen. It was a joy to see the two of them together. They were playful like a newly married couple, something you would not expect from people such as they, whom one would expect to be more sophisticated. It was that simplicity and joy of childhood that made them dear to Joshua. He was that way, in spite of who he was.

Daniel was having a time trying to mash the potatoes. He had already spilled half of them on the counter.

"Daniel," Jana said, laughing, "I can see why you do the paperwork and let others do the real work at your construction sites. Otherwise, the place would be a mess. There'd be cement all over the place. But what you lack in neatness you more than make up for in good intentions. I still love you, dear."

"I'm sorry I can't say the same for you, honey."

"What did you mean by that remark?" she said in a hurt tone of voice.

"Well, what you have in good will is more than matched by your accomplishments, so I can't find anything about you that's negative. Now don't you think that's a compliment?"

"Oh, Dan, you still say such nice things. It is so nice of you to say that."

Supper was a happy experience. They were just glad to see one another. The conversation was light. Joshua's very personal humor startled them with his intimate knowledge of each of them.

After supper Dan offered to help with the dishes; so did Joshua, but Jana and Charlene insisted they go in the den and talk and leave them, as they wanted to prepare the dessert.

"Joshua, I shared your dreams with my staff and asked for their opinions. You might be interested to know that they did not think them as far out as I had originally thought. In fact, some of them thought that from a sociological point of view your ideas were brilliant, and a stroke of public relations genius, which God knows I need badly. From the financial angel, that was different. They wondered how much money I was willing to lose. When they explained in detail I saw their point, and told them I had a longer-range plan than just the one you proposed. I would recoup my losses from an adjacent luxury project I would construct afterward, once the area was rehabilitated and would not appear threatening. My people intend to go over your ideas in more detail and present me with a more complete estimate of what would be involved. I think we might be able to go ahead with it, but you will have to be patient with me because planning for such a project will not be simple. I will have to hire extra teams of architects and engineers and other experts to shorten the timetable."

"I realize that, Daniel, and I am happy you are willing to tackle a project with so many difficult obstacles. But you will not be disappointed. When it is finished you will be able to take an honest pride in the great contribution you have made to the well-being of the community. It will be more important than any other work you have accomplished and will better the lives of thousands of people."

"I hope so because it does make me a bit nervous. But it is a challenge I look forward to, and if you work with me and share your ideas as we go along, I know we can see it to completion. I have to admit, Joshua, that for a man who knows nothing about planning or construction you sure have a remarkable ability to dream up the impossible and make it appear practical."

Joshua was resigned to the fact that the project would take a long time to plan, design, and implement. He was willing to wait, knowing that in the meantime there were many things he could do to prepare the people in the area for the project.

After dessert and coffee, the girls retired and left the two men talking far into the night. Before they went to bed Joshua could see Daniel was already beginning to show enthusiasm for the idea and, in fact, couldn't wait to begin.

X

For weeks Joshua wandered through the neighborhood, meeting with friends he had already made, encountering others who needed his presence. Jeremy had been trying hard to give up drugs but had failed miserably, to the heartbreak of his mother, who had tried in vain to help him. Reluctantly, she was forced ultimately to conclude that it was Jeremy's problem and not hers, so she could worry and pray and storm heaven with her pleading, but unless he was ready to accept God's grace there was absolutely nothing she could do to help him. Even Jennie, who had gone through so much and was now strong and making great progress, was unable to help him. He was not ready. It was only a horrible tragedy that occurred one night that finally shook him back to reality and made him realize he was flirting with death. The panic opened his heart to God's grace and gave him the courage he needed to admit his weakness, and take steps to overcome it, and finally find peace.

It was a dreary night. Jeremy had slipped out of the house without telling anyone. His mother missed him almost immediately and had a horrible premonition of impending calamity. These occurrences were for her nightmares and had the same effect as if the tragedy itself had already struck. The worst part of it was that she was helpless. She did not know where he was or who he was with or what kind of danger he was in. Her fears assumed the worst, her imagination conjuring up one nightmare after another. She could not sleep. She walked the floors trying to distract herself so she would not go out of her mind.

At two o'clock in the morning the phone rang. It was the hospital. Did she have a son named Jeremy? "Yes, yes, what happened? Is he alive? Is he all right?"

"We are not quite sure, ma'am. The doctors are still working on him. He is here in the emergency room in a coma. His legs are broken and his skull is fractured. He has been badly beaten. I know it is late, but you might want to come over."

"Yes, of course," Georgeanne said. "I'll be right there."

Leaving a note on the kitchen table should any of the children wake up, she called a taxi and ran out of the house. In less than fifteen minutes she was at the hospital, frantically looking for her son. When she finally found him, the staff had him cleaned up, so he did not look as bad as he had when the ambulance brought him in.

"Doctor, will he live? How badly is he hurt? Is he still in a coma? Will you be able to put him back together again?"

"Ma'am, we are doing the best we can," the doctor said, trying to be patient. "He has been severely beaten, and we won't know how bad the injuries are until we have had a chance to monitor his condition for a few days. Then we'll have a better understanding of how serious are his injuries. In the meantime, just pray."

She stayed with him all through the night. He was still in a coma by morning and through the following day. On the fourth day he began to show signs of improvement. He could open his eyes and follow people's movements around the room. He could respond to simple instructions by moving his hands or his fingers.

One morning on her way to church Georgeanne met Joshua and poured out her heart to him.

"What am I going to do? Sometimes I think I am going out of my mind worrying about that boy," she said to him. "I often ask myself why you weren't there to help him and prevent this from happening."

"Georgeanne, what happened had to happen. Jeremy was not listening to my Father's voice. His stubbornness was blocking the flow of God's grace. The Holy Spirit always respects people's freedom, but sometimes there is little we can do until a person is finished living, then they will have ears to hear and eyes to see. But God was watching over him, so nothing really tragic happened. Worse things could have happened. What did happen was more dramatic than tragic. So don't worry. The worst is over. Jeremy has finally reached a point where he will be willing to listen. You'll see a big difference from now on, so thank God and be at peace."

"Joshua, I can't tell you how peaceful you make me feel. I guess this is what you were talking about when you met Jeremy the first time, and said he wasn't yet ready to listen to God's grace. Hopefully, this will make him realize he can't live the way he feels. I hope you can stop over to our house sometime, Joshua. You are a blessing to all of us. Jennie asks for you all the time. She is a completely changed girl. The other children you helped that day are still doing well. I really have become a mother to them. It's a comfort to me as well. They are the nicest kids. I think, as you said, their lives were just devoid of love and no one ever cared for them. Now they get all the love they could want. One of the kids' mother died, and it was so beautiful seeing how all the others rallied around and comforted the boy, and brought food to their house so the family would have enough for all the friends and relatives who came visiting. They were so caring, just like a real Joshua family. They love you, Joshua, and they try to do everything the way they think you would like them to. There is a big change in them. I wish you could come to visit them someday."

"I'll be there sometime this week. Tell them I am thinking of them and praying for them. I want them always to be happy, for that is why my Father created them."

Leaving Georganne, Joshua walked over toward the river and sat on the bank, watching the water and the birds and the boats floating up and down. Every now and then a horn blasted, casting, like magic, a mood over the waters. Joshua sat motionless drinking in the scene, sensing the Spirit's presence hovering over the beautiful river and the nearby hills. It was the way he prayed best. It was the way in which his Father spoke to him and guided him, and the reason why his life seemed so well coordinated and orderly, and always so tranquil. It was at times like this that he prayed for all his friends and for Daniel's project, and for those whom he would meet that day. Many as his acquaintances were, each one was a friend and each one was special, and each one knew it. And when he prayed his vast mind encompassed them all, individually.

After almost an hour he left and wandered uptown into another neighborhood. Walking along the street, he encountered two people with long beards and black hats and black suits. As they passed he greeted them in Hebrew but they acted as if they had not heard him. Joshua stopped, noticing they had dropped something, picked a notepad off the sidewalk, then turned and called in Hebrew, "Samuel, I think you dropped this notepad."

The two men turned and looked back, surprised.

Not immediately extending the notepad, Joshua introduced himself. "My name is Joshua," he said in Hebrew.

Being seemingly shy, they did not respond, so Joshua, determined to get them to communicate with him, waited, then continued, "Which of you is Samuel?"

They were impressed with his grasp of Hebrew. The one man answered, "I am Samuel. My companion's name is Moishe."

"Have you lived in this area all your life?" Joshua asked.

"No," Samuel replied. I came from Russia, Moishe is from Poland. We are studying here. Where did you learn such perfect Hebrew?"

"From my parents," Joshua answered.

"In the city?"

"No, in Galilee."

"You are one of us?"

"Yes."

The men's eyes sparkled as they began to show an interest in him.

"Where did you live, and how long ago did you live there?"

"It was a long time ago, and I left home as a young man and traveled, trying to bring the good news of God's love to people."

As they were talking, Joshua casually extended his hand and gave the notepad to Samuel.

They continued talking for a while longer, and, as Joshua showed an interest in the two men, they invited him to visit their synagogue sometime and meet their friends. He could share his experiences of the Holy Land with the community. They would be very happy to welcome him.

"Thank you. I will do that sometime very soon," Joshua assured them.

After thanking Joshua for the notepad, the two men turned and continued on their way.

It was a beautiful summer afternoon. Joshua wandered farther uptown, meeting different kinds of people along the way.

A young blond-haired boy was leading three others to a Salvation Army shop. Joshua could hear their conversation as they were close by. The three men were troubled souls and not able to function well. The blond boy had sensed they were disoriented and offered to help them.

"Come, I will show you where you can get a bite to eat. Also, there is a place nearby where you can buy your clothes cheap."

Joshua smiled at the young boy's concern for the three men, who clearly had difficulty living in the real world.

Later on, Joshua encountered the blond boy again.

"Hello, young man! I saw what you did earlier for those three men. That was very kind of you."

A little embarrassed and nervous at being approached by the stranger, the boy smiled timidly and said, "Thank you."

"My name is Joshua. What is yours?"

"George."

"That's a good name. You have a real godly spirit, George, and a pure, innocent soul," Joshua told him.

The boy said nothing, just looked at Joshua, wondering about him, and beginning to feel uncomfortable with this stranger who was intruding on his privacy, and saying all kinds of nice things when he did not even know him.

"Not everyone is innocent or sincere. Be careful whom you trust and embrace as friends," Joshua told him. "Talk to God when you are hurting and confused or feel alone. He is always by your side as your friend. He loves you immensely."

Joshua reached out and shook the boy's hand, then continued on his way. It was almost noon.

Encountering students from a nearby university, he greeted them as they walked past. Some were friendly, others ignored him. As he approached the campus he was struck by the illusion of peace and serenity created by the sprawling lawn and the carefully kept gardens. Walking through the gate and along the path, he spotted a vacant bench and sat down to rest.

Students were coming and going like bees around a hive, often walking in small groups discussing classwork or professors' theories, excited about the new world of knowledge that had suddenly burst in upon their young minds only waiting to be explored.

Joshua watched curiously as they walked by, absorbed in their private worlds. They came in all shapes and forms and colors, wearing clothes of every imaginable design. But it was not the clothes that attracted Joshua. He was intrigued by what he could see beneath the surface of each of their lives: their dreams, their fears, their joys, the nightmares so many carried with them from childhood, the ill-concealed fright in the eyes of those who lived on the edge of panic and despair. He would have liked to reach out to them and heal them, but the doors of their hearts were closed and not ready to accept what he had to give. That is the ever present ache in the heart of God, seeing the pain in people's lives and being unable to help because He is unwanted, and knowing He can never violate the freedom He has given us.

As he sat basking in the warm spring sunshine, a Doberman pinscher broke loose from his keeper and pranced over to him, and began sniffing at his sandals. Joshua reached over and petted the animal. An embarrassed young lady came to retrieve the dog. "Come here, Otto!"

But the dog ignored her and continued to sniff at Joshua's clothes. The girl apologized profusely, but he looked up and smiled.

"No need to apologize," he said. "Otto is a perfectly normal dog who enjoys meeting people."

"He is a good dog, but has his own mind," the girl continued. "He's supposed to be my guard dog. I live in a bad neighborhood where it is dangerous to walk alone, especially for a woman, so my father bought Otto to be my companion. My name, by the way, is Harriet. I go to school here. I'm a biochemistry major."

"My name is Joshua. I also live in the neighborhood. I walked in here for the peace and quiet, and to rest for a while."

"Do you attend classes here?"

"No, I never had the good fortune to attend a school like this."

While they talked, Otto played with Joshua's hand, making believe he was going to bite him, trying to get Joshua to play with him.

"Is that dog being a pest?"

"No, not at all. Why don't you sit down here and rest until Otto finishes chewing my hand?"

Harriet was glad to talk to someone, and began telling Joshua about her family and where they lived.

"I came halfway across the country to go to school here. This is my third year, and I love it. The only thing I don't like is the cramped neighborhood around here. I am so used to the wide outdoors. My family owns a farm and we have over twenty thousand acres. Some of it is grazing land, and the rest we farm. I love the wide-open spaces and the beautiful sunsets. About the only time you see the sun around here is at high noon when it is right above your head."

"It must be a happy place to live," Joshua exclaimed.

"It is and I can't wait for classes to end so I can go home and breathe in the cool, fresh air. Even the manure in the fields will smell good. But I'll probably be back to take summer classes anyway. There are some courses I still need."

"What are you preparing for, Harriet?"

"I'm taking biochemistry and genetics. I want to do genetic engineering when I graduate."

"That's a new field of research. It must be challenging to a young student."

"I love it. There are so many possibilities for curing illnesses and for correcting genetic defects in situations that seemed hopeless before."

"Life was so beautiful when it came from the heart of God. So many problems have sprung up and so many accidents have occurred through the long span of creation. Careless use of nature's gifts and abuse of the environment have severely damaged this beautiful masterpiece my Father designed. Scientists can correct many of the mistakes, and now even the accidents that have damaged our genetic structure.

"But this kind of work is fragile and sensitive. Humble people who have no need to play God can best do this work. Left to the arrogant with no morals, it can do more damage to the human race and to nature than an atomic bomb. A scientist can be a genius, but also a moral infant with no sensitivity to monsters they can create. Frankenstein was not just a nightmare. He is only too real in our modern world, a genius with no conscience, for whom life is just a toy. Human life is sacred, and it must be treated as sacred from its very first spark. We will one day answer for how we handled life. It is a privilege to be allowed to be a partner with God in perfecting His creation. It must be done humbly and prayerfully, because in this you share the power of God Himself in fashioning the destiny of humanity."

"Gee, you really feel strongly about this, don't you?" Harriet said, surprised.

"Yes, Harriet, and with good reason. There are a lot of people with sick minds, and just because they are scientists, it doesn't mean they are morally or psychologically healthy. This fragile work should be carefully monitored."

"You should come to one of our classes and talk to us sometime," Harriet interjected. "One of our professors is the sensitive kind you talk about. He would be thrilled to meet you. One of our other professors is an idiot. I don't know how he ever got a job teaching young people, who are so impressionable. One or two of the students like him, but they think just the way he does. Genetics for them is just a game. They are going to cause a lot of trouble someday."

Getting up to leave, Harriet attached the leash to Otto. "It has been a pleasure meeting you, Joshua. I hope our paths cross again sometime. I enjoyed listening to you. Your vision is so clear. We need that kind of focus."

"Enjoy your studies, Harriet, and God bless you and your family."

Later in the day Joshua stopped to see his friends in the furniture business. By now they had a shop where they did all their work. They were also able to purchase a pickup truck, which was a big help and doubled their business. He arrived at the shop just as they were finishing a sofa and were about ready to quit for the day.

"Well, look who walks in when the work is all done. You might know, always just in time for supper," Elijah shouted to his brother, as Joshua came walking through the door.

"Do you blame me? Can you tell me where I can find a better cook than your mother? I wasn't born yesterday, you know. Until you find someone who can cook better than your mother, you're stuck with me."

"Where did you get those flowers, man? Did you snitch them from somebody's yard?" Elijah asked with a wide toothy grin, as he spotted the bouquet Joshua was carrying. "I know you're bringing them for Mama. You really like her, don't you, man?"

"She's one special mother, and you boys better not forget it," Joshua shot back. "I brought flowers for you to give her. It wouldn't be a bad idea for you to do it occasionally. Little things mean a lot to a mother. How is your business? I can see your brother is working hard as usual."

"Man, I been working twice as hard as he has. He just always looks like he's working. You just happen to show up whenever I'm taking a rest."

"No matter when I come, right? Amazing!"

"He did work hard today, Joshua," Gordon interrupted. "I have to admit it. I don't know what I would have done without him. We have been so busy. And you'd be surprised, he's a better craftsman than I am. I hate to admit that, too, but it's true. He's just a motor mouth. I'd get ear plugs if I wasn't afraid of missing phone calls."

"Gordon, man, you ain't never had it so good. This place would be dead if I wasn't around here. You got it made, man. Hurry up, brother, it's past suppertime, and Joshua's hungry, I can tell. I don't know why. All he does is walk around the neighborhood all day, just glad-handin' everybody. He's got it made, one happy freeloadin' dude. He's as free as a bird and everybody takes care of him. That's the way to live, man."

"Nobody could afford my services, so I just let them treat me," Joshua shot back in good humor.

Joshua enjoyed Elijah's humor. It was quick and sharp and affectionate. It was really his way of expressing how glad he was to see Joshua. A lot different from the way he used to ignore him in the beginning. Joshua loved him.

The three cleaned up the shop, Joshua sweeping the floor, Elijah putting the rolls of material away, and Gordon gathering together all the receipts for the day. Then the three men got into the truck and Gordon drove home.

"Mama, guess who we brought home for supper tonight?" Elijah blurted out as soon as he opened the door to the apartment. "Our one and only, never-late-for-supper guest, Joshua."

"Elijah, you behave yourself. Joshua knows he's welcome here any time he likes," his mother hollered back at him.

"Mama, look what Gordon and I brought you," Elijah said as he gave his mother the flowers, waiting for her to kiss him.

"Oh, thank you, boys, you are so thoughtful," Josephine said as she reached out to kiss both of them.

Gordon grinned, telling his mother, "Joshua's the one you should kiss. He brought the flowers into the store so we could give them to you. But we paid him for them. We bought him a Coke on the way home."

"Well, you are all very thoughtful," she said as she kissed Joshua too. "Now let's get down to business. You're already late, so hurry and get washed up and by the time you're ready the supper will be on the table."

Joshua was the first one finished washing. He sat at the table and talked with Josephine.

"Joshua, what a marked change in those boys. They are so different now that they have a sense of pride in all they have been accomplishing. Their business is growing so fast. They have orders already for the next two months. Gordon is turning out to be a good businessman. He's good with numbers and keeps accurate records. He's been taking a night course in bookkeeping for the past week and likes it very much. It's a big help in the business.

"The two of them decided last night to hire employees to catch up with the backlog. I hope they get people who are trustworthy."

"I wouldn't worry," Joshua told her. "They are sharp young men, and they know the streets and they can pretty well size up people. They'll choose wisely."

Supper was fun, but Gordon noticed the empty place. "I wish Sis would come home sometime at least to visit. It's not the same without her."

"She'll be back when she's ready. Just pray for her," Joshua said.

Everyone was hungry and ate well, to Josephine's delight.

XI

DURING THE WEEK Joshua sent word to Georgeanne that he would stop for a visit on Sunday morning, and said it would be nice if the whole "family" could be there. When he showed up on Sunday he got quite a reception. Georgeanne's whole "family" was there, including the ones she had adopted after the cult service that dramatic Sunday morning.

They were all sitting around the living room patiently waiting for his arrival. The huge welcome that greeted him when he entered was overwhelming. Josephine motioned for him to sit in the place they had reserved for him. Sitting down, he spoke to them: "I am so happy to be with you all this morning. Even though we do not see each other very often, you are always on my mind and in my heart. You are very dear to me.

"I have heard that you all have jobs now and have been helping one another. That is the way families should be. I am proud of you. I wish you would share with me some of the things that are happening in your lives. I am sure we can all benefit from it."

Jennie was the first to speak. "Joshua, Jeremy has so much to tell you, but he's embarrassed to start. Give him a little encouragement, would you?"

"Jennie, you really embarrass me now. I'll speak when I feel comfortable with it," Jeremy shot back.

"Jennie," Joshua spoke up, "Jeremy is right. When he's ready, he'll tell us.

"You are not reluctant to share with us, Jeremy, are you?"

"No, Joshua, it's not that. It's just that it's hard for me to get it all straight in my head so it will come out right. Too many things have happened in the past few weeks; it is hard to put it all into words. Like the night I was taken to the hospital. I hardly remember what happened that night. All I know is I woke up in the hospital. I heard what the doctors and everybody was saying, and I knew what was going on but I was out of it. I guess I was in a coma. I heard the doctors saying that there was no way I was going to make it. I was frightened, but I was determined I was going to get better. I prayed during the coma. I didn't pray with my lips. I had no control over anything. I just prayed with my heart, and I knew God was listening to me. I felt His peace come over me and I knew I would be all right. I knew I was in some kind of a state, but I could not reach outside myself. I knew it was a coma because everyone was talking about a coma. When Mom came in, she was frantic. I wanted to talk to her and tell her I was going to be all right, but I couldn't speak and I couldn't communicate. I prayed hard those four days, like I never prayed before. When I came out of the coma and started to get better, I knew God had answered all my prayers. I guess I was finally ready to listen to Him and set my life straight. When I got out of the hospital, I never wanted to see a drug again. I had an intense aversion to them. Thank God. None of the terrible craving that was so cruel and so demanding. Just an inner peace that God was with me, and with that peace a greater high than I had ever experienced before. I wish I could share that with all the others who are still hooked and troubled and searching."

"That was remarkable, Jeremy," Joshua said.

Jeremy did not even realize that he was telling so simply and so powerfully what had happened to him, and without the slightest self-consciousness.

Joshua looked at Jennie and smiled. She smiled back, impressed with the sly way Joshua was able to nudge Jeremy into telling his story, without even realizing it.

"Joshua," Georgeanne said, "I really don't have too terribly much to say, except that I finally understand what it means to trust God. When I was worrying so much, you told me not to worry. I said to myself, 'It's easy for him to say that, he doesn't have a care in the world, and no one to worry about, except himself.' Then I thought about what you said and I began to realize, slowly and not all at once, that worrying does not really accomplish anything except to drive us crazy. The more I thought about what you said, the more it made sense to me. If God is real, as I believe He is, then He is concerned about me and about my loved ones. When I talk to Him and share with Him my concerns, He must listen and, as a loving Father, He will not turn away from a heart that is breaking. Each day I think of that and each day I find myself trusting Him more and worrying less. Sometimes I get panic attacks, but they are less frequent.

"Joshua, you are so right, God does care and He does involve Himself in our lives. Something much worse could have happened to Jeremy that night, but it didn't. Now he is well on the mend, thank God. Joshua, that brings me to another matter that weighs heavily on my mind. I hope you don't mind if I ask you. All the while Jeremy was going through his crisis, you seemed to be aware of everything that was happening to him, and even his state of mind. It makes me wonder who you really are beneath that simple facade. Sometimes I get the strangest feeling that you are God come down to help us. I have thought that ever since the day with the devil worshipers when they all got so frightened when you entered the room."

An eerie silence followed Georgeanne's sharing of her feelings. Everyone's eyes were on Joshua. He sat there deep in thought and, after a few moments, merely said, "Georgeanne, God is never far from any of us. Always remember that. You are never alone."

Knowing that Joshua wanted to shift away from the subject, Georgeanne politely moved to another topic.

"Marisa," Georgeanne said, "I've been watching you and I know you can't wait to share what has happened to you recently. Why don't you tell us all? I am sure Joshua would be thrilled to hear it."

Marisa was one of the girls healed during the devil-worship service.

"I'm embarrassed, Georgeanne, but I'll try anyway. It's hard for me to speak in front of a group. . . . Joshua, ever since that day—you know the one I mean. Ever since that day, I have been different. Georgeanne and everyone has been so kind to me. They have become the family I never had. I guess that was why I was attracted to that awful group in the first place, because I had no one, and I thought they would be family to me. Well, ever since that day, Joshua, when you freed me, I have had such peace. I can't begin to describe it. My new family have been a real source of strength to me. I have never known such love and such caring, and it is not phony either. It is real. Well, this past week something happened that I just can't believe. I had been feeling that I was a real drag on my family because I didn't have a job, and everyone was supporting me. I had tried to get a job, but no matter where I went, I was not what they were looking for. Finally, when I was almost desperate, I applied for this job at the newspaper. It was just a simple job, running errands for anybody and everybody, which required no talent or education whatever.

"I was sitting outside the office of the person who was doing the hiring. I had been waiting for at least forty-five minutes, when a lady walked by. I was just sitting there doodling on a pad the secretary gave me to calm my nerves. I guess she could see I was a wreck. Well, this lady saw me doodling as she passed by. She stopped, then turned around and asked if she could see what I was doing. I gave her the pad. She looked at it for a few moments, then looked at me and asked if she could see me in her office. The secretary told her I was waiting to be interviewed by her supervisor. The lady must have been important because she merely said, 'Tell him I wanted to talk with her.'

"When she brought me to her office she asked me all kinds of questions about myself, about what kind of art work I do, about where I worked before. I was honest with her. I told her I only went to high school, that I had no training in art but just drew everything in sight since I was a child. I told her I had never had a job before except for part-time jobs at fast food places. She asked me to draw some things for her right on the spot. I did them. She was impressed at how fast I could draw things and how perfect they looked.

"Then she said she was going to start a special series of articles on plants and animals common around the city and the surrounding areas, so people could become familiar with the plant and animal life around them. She asked me to draw some sample pictures of a few complicated plants, which I did, and a squirrel's head, which I did. She seemed real impressed and offered me the job to do all the artwork for the series of articles. She said if I do well on the series she will hire me full time. Starting salary she offered was thirty thousand dollars. I almost fainted. I don't know what she saw in me, but she was a gift from God."

When Marisa looked at Joshua, he was smiling at her, which gave her the distinct impression he already knew all about it, which made her also wonder how and what he could have had to do with it. Knowing what was going through her mind, Joshua said, "See, Marisa, how God notices every little happening in your life, and how much you needed Him that day. He always makes things happen when we need Him."

"Joshua," Jennie broke in, "I have a question that has been bothering me ever since that horrible Sunday morning. When we worshiped Satan during those services, why did the leader always use bread and wine and imitate a priest at a Mass?"

"Devil worshipers have done that for centuries. Those rituals are called Black Masses. Sometimes they have one of their disciples sneak into a church during Mass and take Communion with the others, then put it in their pocket and bring it to their devil-worship service. They then perform obscene rituals around the consecrated bread as a way of showing their hatred of Jesus, by mocking Him in what they know to be His sacred presence. It drives the devils to frenzy."

"Joshua," Georgeanne asked, "why can't we have Communion? Jesus promised it in the gospels and told the apostles to do it. We never have it except at church. Do you think we could have Jesus' Communion sometime?"

"Georgeanne, Jesus is always present with you. He is always by your side. He instituted the breaking of bread as a more intimate expression of His presence to assure His followers of His closeness, especially during difficult times, and to deepen His life within them. Yes, if you like, we could have Eucharist, right now if you would like to. Eucharist is a perfect way of thanking God through Jesus. That is what the word itself means, Thanksgiving."

"What do we do?" Georgeanne asked.

"Just get a glass with enough wine in it for everyone and a roll or a piece of bread and put it here on the coffee table."

Georgeanne did as directed.

As everyone sat back and relaxed, Joshua began speaking to them and explained what he was about to do. Everyone sat in rapt attention.

"At the Last Supper, Jesus knew His apostles would be devastated by His leaving them, so He wanted to give them the assurance that He would be present with them always in a very special way, like the way Yahweh made Himself specially present to Moses in the burning bush, and to the Israelites in the show bread preserved in the Temple, and to Elijah in the gentle breeze. Jesus' love is very tender, and in that tenderness He wants us to know that we are never alone but that He is always with us. And so, at the end of the Passover meal on the night before He died, He took the bread, broke it, gave it to His disciples, saying to them, 'Take this and eat it. This is my body.' Then He took the cup of wine, blessed it, and gave it to them, saying, 'Take this, all of you, and drink of it. This is the cup of my blood which will be shed for all of you for the forgiveness of sins. Do this in my memory.'

"In doing this, Jesus gave them a precious heritage, a way of assuring them of His constant presence. 'Whoever eats this bread abides in me and I in him,' he told them. This presence, smuggled into the prisons, was a great comfort to the early martyrs in the Roman prisons.

"As we prepare to receive the body and blood of Jesus, we pray to the Father in the words Jesus taught His apostles: 'Our Father, who art in heaven.' " They all began to pray together. " 'Hallowed be your name. Your kingdom come. Your will be done on earth as it is in heaven. Give us this day our daily bread and forgive us our sins as we forgive those who sin against us. And lead us not into temptation, but deliver us from the Evil One.' "

Then Joshua lifted his eyes to heaven and prayed quietly for a few moments. It was the first time they had seen him pray. They watched him in awe. They could tell by the transfigured look on his face that he was communicating with the Father. Lowering his eyes, he picked up the bread roll and blessed it. Then, looking around at each one, he said, "And I say to you now, this is my body. Take it and eat it," as he broke the bread roll in half and passed it to those on either side.

Then, taking the glass of wine, he blessed it and said, "Take this cup and drink of it, all of you. This is the cup of my blood which is shed for you for the forgiveness of sins."

He then passed the cup for them all to drink.

As they sat in quiet thanksgiving, Joshua prayed in a quiet voice, "Father, You have formed us all into a little family caring for one another. They have come here this morning in my name and now are one with me, Father. When You look into their hearts, see myself in them, Father, and bless them and keep them from harm. They now pray to You and offer their thanks to You through my presence within them which has consecrated them in Your love. Be always with them, Father, so their whole lives will be a living thanksgiving for all that You have done for them. May they bring Your love and Your peace to all they meet. And may they know always the joy and peace of Your sacred presence within them."

Then, spontaneously, Georgeanne started singing, " 'Alleluia, Alleluia, Alleluia. Give the glory and the honor to the Lord,' " as the others joined in, singing the rest of the hymn with her.

When they finished singing, everyone sat still for a few moments, just looking at Joshua, wondering, and now knowing, but not daring to ask any questions. He smiled at them reassuringly, and they knew for sure. Their awe of him now knew no bounds. They now saw God as so humble and unfrightening.

"What I have shared with you is for yourselves," he told them. "You must keep it among yourselves and tell no one."

Georgeanne picked up the glass and the dish and took them back out into the kitchen, washing them out and hiding them in a special place. They would be forever special to her.

The group broke up around noon. Joshua walked through the park, enjoying the animals and birds, and the carefully kept gardens that always gave him such pleasure. Later in the afternoon he went down to the Trumbulls.

XII

THE TRUMBULLS HAD been expecting Joshua, and as usual were thrilled to see him, though each time he came, of late, he spent more and more time talking to Daniel, who was totally immersed in the Joshua project. Daniel was only beginning to fathom the vastness of the undertaking and, as his awareness grew, his awe of Joshua increased immeasurably.

"What a mind this man must have!" he said to Jana and Charlene one night on returning from work. "The architects and engineers are overwhelmed at the immensity of the project and how it embraces every aspect of people's lives. Joshua forgot nothing, nothing, not the slightest detail. The depth and breadth of his vision are uncanny. Even the most complex ideas he reduces to simplicity. Only when the engineers dissect his concepts and analyze them do they begin to realize the implications. Sometimes they wonder if he is really aware of all that's involved. But *I* know he is *fully* aware, and that's what is so awesome, how a man can grasp so many intricate details at one time and never get rattled or even confused."

In response, Jana said, "Daniel, I have the feeling God sent that man into our lives for a special reason. Don't you feel a sense of peace whenever he's with us? I know I do."

"Yes, he seems to affect everyone that way. He sure has been a gift to us."

That evening at the Trumbulls' was Joshua's last for many weeks. He was nowhere to be seen by any of his friends. They were all doing well, and probably did not need him anyway. Josephine and her family were doing well. Georgeanne and her extended family were thriving, and were a great source of strength and joy to one another as well as to others in the neighborhood. Two of the young people in Georgeanne's new "family" were white, but that made no difference; they were accepted and treated with as much love as the others.

Joshua's two Hasidic acquaintances were surprised when he showed up at their synagogue one Friday evening for the service. Of course, he stood out in the crowd, the only one who was not wearing a black suit and fedora, and a black beard. He was not well received when he first arrived at the gathering in front of the synagogue, but when Moishe and Samuel excitedly ran over and greeted him, everyone thought he was a long-lost relative, especially when they heard the Hebrew flow like honey from his lips. They were all then very impressed, because most of the others spoke only various versions of Yiddish. His Hebrew was an old dialect, which made them wonder where he had learned it and where he came from, but it was impressive nonetheless.

After the initial warm greetings, the mood turned somber. Their gathering that evening was a sad one. Their beloved Rebbe had just died and his passing devastated all his followers. Many of them had placed great stock in that man. They thought for sure he was the anointed one sent by Yahweh. Now he was gone. Talk among some was that he might rise again, but they were encouraged by other respected rabbis not to place their hope in that. If God wanted it, it would happen, but even the Rebbe himself had not even mentioned such a thing, so there was no foundation in reality for even considering the idea.

The service itself was subdued. A sadness, a melancholy hung like a mist on a hot, sultry day. The prayers were all said with deep reverence and devotion. When the dead were all remembered, the Rebbe was given special mention and all prayed for the peace of his soul and thanked God for all the time he had spent with them interpreting so faithfully God's message to everyone. He was truly a prophet in his day, not just to Jews but to all who would listen and hear the word of God.

After the service, a small group of Moishe's and Samuel's friends surrounded Joshua and asked if he knew the Rebbe.

"I knew him very well," Joshua replied to their questioning.

"What did you think of him?" was their next question.

"He was an extraordinarily sincere man, intent on understanding what was the will of God. He was uncompromising in his devotion to God's will, and he communicated that zeal to all his loyal disciples. He had many times more followers than even Gamaliel had in his day. He is now at peace with God and is alive forever in my Father's presence."

The crowd was taken aback when he said the words "my Father's presence." They did not understand what he meant by it.

"Where do we look for the Messiah now?" one of them asked.

"Keep your eyes and your minds open, and you will find him. Do not look for him or you will end up creating your own Messiah. Be sincere in allowing Yahweh's light to enter your hearts and He will lead you to him in His own good time. But do not be anxious. Be patient, be prayerful, and be open to Yahweh's will. He will speak to you and guide you.

Be good people. Care for others, not just your own. They are also the children of Yahweh, all created with tender love. Your love should be like His love, nonexclusive, and your vision, as well as your hearts, will expand to the measure of His all-embracing concern."

Joshua and Moishe and Samuel walked together and eventually arrived at Moishe's house, where they just sat on the front steps and talked until late. It was a hot evening and Moishe's wife, Anna, brought out cold drinks for everyone but did not stay. Joshua talked to her briefly, even though he knew it was not considered proper, and after a few minutes she excused herself and went back inside.

Though Joshua had not visited his friends during that time, he still wandered through the extended neighborhood, talking to people as he walked along. Seeing into people's souls, he knew their pain and their anguish. When he spoke to them, they immediately knew he understood and felt drawn to him. Before long they ended up pouring their hearts out to him. When they walked away, it was with a peace and a comfort they had never known.

There was also a practical objective to Joshua's working the neighborhood. He knew the people would have to be prepared for the development project. It was his dream that they should all share in making the project work. To do this they had to be part of it. They had to be supportive of it. They had to be taught that, as God's children, they should learn to think in terms of others in their community, not just themselves and what they wanted to get out of life. There was a profound theological dimension to Dan Trumbull's undertaking, as Joshua conceived it. People had to be prepared for it and share in the vision and be caught up in the idea that this could be something that could change the lives of a whole community. For this, however, they would have to rise above their own petty world and share in a vision that embraced the dreams and needs of everyone around them. They would have to develop a genuine interest in the welfare of the whole surrounding community. Some rare few had already arrived at that level of goodness. For most it would be a totally foreign way of thinking. Joshua knew it would not be easy to teach them to think differently. He also knew that, with patience and dogged persistence, he would change their way of thinking. Being able to work together to accomplish a common goal for the community, and in the process better the lives of everyone, particularly the children, was a sublime proof of the sincerity of their love of God. Joshua's role, as he saw it, was to teach them how to expand the vision of their lives and add a new dimension to their dreams. To accomplish this he traveled the length and breadth of the community, talking to individuals along the streets and meeting with them in gatherings large and small.

He never talked about the project as such. That was Daniel Trumbull's job. He did, however, discuss the possibility of changes in the community, and sparked their imaginations over how things could be if only someone was interested. He painted a picture for them of what an ideal community could be like, a community not unlike the one that Daniel and his colleagues were developing on their drawing boards and in their computers. By the time he had pretty well covered the whole community with his promotion work, architects' renderings of the project were beginning to appear at strategic places throughout the community. News announcements about the project emphasized the vastness of the undertaking, and the fact that the developers wanted the people in the community to share in the work on the project, since it would be their neighborhood. Plans were being made to provide temporary housing for those who would be displaced until the residential part of the project was completed.

People in the community were awed by the beauty of the project and could not believe that they would one day live in a place so beautiful. There were tree-lined streets and parks. The houses were not huge high-rises, but one- to four-family houses. Senior housing was partially scattered, partially clustered, so people could have options. Clinics spaced strategically throughout the neighborhoods and subsidized by pharmaceutical companies were particularly attractive for people with children. This idea was Jana's contribution to the project.

The concept of industries and schools forming partnerships in which young people who were not destined for college could still prepare for life excited the imagination even of the children. That industry could recognize the talent of those whom schools ordinarily overlooked or cast aside made the young people feel for the first time in their young lives that there was hope. The dream of having their talents developed and being taught technical skills, then on graduation being hired by the local factories, excited them.

Joshua's preparing the people for this dream was now paying off. Daniel's public relations teams scheduled community meetings at regular intervals to paint an overall picture of the project and then explain details and answer questions. People could not wait for the daily newspapers to come out so they could follow every phase as it unfolded. They could not believe that they would be trained and hired to do the actual construction work. Even though it would take a long time before the whole project was in full swing, training could start reasonably soon, and then demolition not long afterward. Daniel already owned much of the real estate in the area, so whole sections were ready for demolition.

Moving families to temporary quarters was a major operation. Daniel had done it before, so he was always prepared for such contingencies. The fact that he owned so many buildings in the vicinity or not very far away made it relatively simple for him to relocate people. His technicians trained a sizable number of men and women from the area to work on the demolition phase. They were slow and inefficient in the beginning, but after a few weeks they were quite expert in handling backhoes, forklifts, bulldozers, and dump trucks, as well as doing the more menial work that was required. It made a big difference in everyone's life. Some of the people abused the windfall of fat paychecks which were so new to them. But most went home to their families proud and with heads held high because they could now finally take care of their families with dignity. On the job, a few were uninspired, but the others, who were mostly relatives or at least neighborhood friends, needled them until they realized what a chance they had. This was the chance of a lifetime for the community. They were determined not to lose it.

XIII

ONE DAY JOSHUA appeared at the demolition site. Daniel was checking on the progress of the work, and when he noticed Joshua he was shocked.

"Joshua, where in creation have you been? I have been sending my men all over town trying to find you, and no one had the slightest idea where you were," Daniel said to him, betraying the exasperation he felt.

There were many details of the plans he wanted to discuss with him, and Joshua's inaccessibility was irritating and incomprehensible. He should have known how critical his presence was, particularly during the beginning stages of a project of such immense proportions.

"I have been around, doing all the public relations work for your project," Joshua responded in a most casual manner, which unsettled Daniel.

"You're so casual about it and I have been tearing at what little hair I have left trying to get in touch with you. Can you come down to my office sometime soon so we can look at the plans together?"

"Yes, that should be fun."

"Fun, you say. We have been sweating over them for months now and you call it fun. Well, I guess from your perspective it probably is. There are so many questions the architects want to ask you."

"When would you like me to be there?"

"Tomorrow, if you can. I'd appreciate it."

"I'll be there. I'm sorry if I made things difficult for you."

"Well, I just did not expect you to disappear the way you did for so long a time. Now that we have found each other again, what do you think of the site?" Daniel asked him, changing the subject.

"I can see things already taking shape. Daniel, it is going to be magnificent. I think you and your team will be proud of what you will have accomplished."

"Don't forget, Jana has also been a part of this project. She is so enthusiastic about it. In fact, it is the first project she has ever worked on with me. She's really enjoying it, and so am I. She has some wonderful suggestions. I'll show you the architects' sketches tomorrow. By the way, before I forget, there is a young man at the office whom I hope you might talk to. He's one of my best engineers but I'm afraid we're going to lose him if he doesn't straighten out. He's heavy into cocaine, and I'm really worried for him. I've known his family all my life. They are such nice people and they are devastated. I don't know what to do. Perhaps you can help the boy. He is a fine young man, but if he doesn't get ahold of himself, I'm afraid he's going to destroy himself and ruin his whole future."

"I'll do what I can, Daniel. Don't worry! Just trust!"

" 'Just trust!' you say. Trust whom? I've been trying to trust you, but when I don't hear from you for weeks, I wonder. I've had to rely on myself all my life. Experience has taught me to trust no one but myself, and now I have to relearn everything since I met you."

Daniel walked Joshua through the site. He was shocked at the number of workers, most of them black or Spanish-speaking, who called out to Joshua. Some of them were driving dump trucks, others running bulldozers or front-end loaders, and some doing the supporting work by helping others.

"Where did you meet all those people? It seems everybody knows you," Daniel asked him in wonderment.

Joshua laughed. "Just wandering around, talking to people."

"You must have made quite an impression. They are obviously delighted to see you. You'd think you were their long-lost friend."

Actually many of them were people Joshua had been talking to the past few months as he tried to prepare people in the neighborhood for what he knew would be happening in their lives. In some subtle way they felt they owed their jobs to him, since he had prepared them for what was going to take place and made them feel comfortable with it. Otherwise, they might not have even been interested in what to them was just another project like all the others from which they had been evicted and relocated.

"Joshua, I have to admit," Daniel said to him as they walked through the site, "when I first committed myself to this project, it was with a certain sense of panic. I knew it would be costly and, from bitter experience with past unforeseen cost overruns, I had a difficult time sleeping. But now that I am well into the program, I can't tell you how much I enjoy it. I somehow feel it is something that is supposed to be done, and the finances, as complicated as they are, will work themselves out."

"Don't worry, Daniel! My Father has His own way of handling finances. When someone makes an effort to help others, He makes sure there will be an abundance of resources. Accountants may predict a deficit, but income will appear from sources you never dreamed of. You cannot outdo God in generosity."

"I am already seeing that. When you first suggested this idea that night at my house, the interest rates at the time were thirteen percent. I held off as long as I could and used some of my own capital. Now the interest rates have fallen to almost nine percent, and it looks like they will drop even lower. Do you know what that means for a project of this size that will eventually cost three billion dollars? A savings of a hundred twenty million dollars a year in interest alone.

"And that's not all. Once the big corporations realized that we were doing this not as a self-serving project, and sensed it could actually succeed, several of them asked if they could provide part of the funding, either for the overall project or for segments of it. They feel it can be the redemption of our cities, and can turn the tide of the plague eating at the innards of our great cities. They want to be part of it.

"And something you will probably be glad to hear: inmates in prisons read about the project in the newspapers and offered their help free of charge, if we could work out an arrangement with the Corrections Department. They said they would be only too happy to make their little contribution to better conditions that made their own lives so miserable when they were growing up. We talked to the officials and they said they would be agreeable to providing work release details on a daily arrangement, that would be carefully supervised by their own officers, and with the understanding that the inmates would go back to prison at night. So far it is working out very well. It has given the men and women a sense of pride they never had before."

"See, Daniel, how God works when we do something

good. 'Everything works together for those who do good,' "
Joshua said to him. "I can tell you are enjoying the project."

"I can't tell you how much. I never realized how good it
feels when you are doing something that can better people's
lives. It is so much better than just accumulating money. To
see the happy look on all those workers' faces when they
come to work in the morning brings joy to my heart. You can
see hope in their eyes. That's worth more than if I just made
ten million dollars. Joshua, since we haven't seen you in so
long, I am sure Jana and Charlene would love to see you
again. Charlene will be going away to school soon. It might
be the last chance you will get to see her before she leaves.
How about next Sunday for dinner?"

"I'm beginning to see why you are such a good
businessman, Daniel. You really know how to make an offer
that is impossible to turn down. I'll be there. Bring them my
peace. And I will see that young man who works at your
office whenever you can arrange it."

"I'll talk to you about it tomorrow. I'll send a driver up
here to pick you up and bring you to my office."

"Good. I'll be here at the site."

Finishing the tour, the two men parted, Daniel walking
off with some of his men, Joshua continuing on his way. It
had been a long time since Joshua had seen Georgeanne or
Josephine and their families. As they lived not far from the
site, he headed in that direction.

A lot had happened while he was away. Gordon and
Elijah had expanded their business twice. They now had
eight employees, five women and three men, one of the men
an Irishman who had just come from the old country, and
was a nephew of the old-timer Joshua had met at the church
when he first arrived in the neighborhood months before.

He spoke with a thick brogue which Elijah managed to imitate with rather good success.

One morning a black customer came into the shop and was talking to Gordon. He heard the strange accent on the other side of the shop and turned around to see who it was and saw Elijah spewing forth with a thick brogue.

"Where's that dude from?" he asked Gordon, bewildered at hearing such a strange sound coming from a black man.

Gordon laughed so hard he could hardly stop. "That's my brother Elijah. He doesn't really talk like that. He's imitating that Irishman over there in the corner. We just hired him last month, and Elijah is obsessed with his brogue. If he doesn't stop, he's going to end up talking like that permanently. He has everyone who comes in here in stitches. To make things worse, the Irishman is learning rap talk, which he speaks with a brogue. I'd like to put them on television."

Just as Joshua was walking into the shop, the customer was walking out shaking his head.

"What a nutty place!" the man said to Joshua.

"Nutty?" Joshua exclaimed.

"Yeah, man, like in fruitcake. Wait till you hear them in there," the man continued, and walked past Joshua.

"Oh, the top o' the marnin' to you, me young man," a voice shouted from the corner when Joshua walked in. And it wasn't the Irishman who said it.

Shocked, Joshua looked over at Gordon, who was just shaking his head in bewilderment.

"You never know what to expect from that brother of yours. What's this new thing with the brogue?" Joshua said as he and Gordon greeted each other with a big, warm hug.

"Don't ask me. I've given up trying to explain him to people. We hired an Irishman last month. He's really a good worker. He did upholstering in Ireland and is good at it. He and my brother are as thick as thieves, inseparable. They're even trying to speak like each other. I don't know which one is nuttier. They're going to drive me crazy if they keep it up much longer. They never stop. Imagine listenin' to that mouth twenty-four hours a day! And now the Irishman. He's just as bad. I could almost swear he's a white double of my brother."

Joshua could not help laughing, even though he could sympathize with Gordon.

"Forget them for a while. Tell me how you—"

"Forget them? Man, how can we forget them? They never shut up. Here they come."

"Joshua, brother, how I missed you, man!" Elijah said as he leapfrogged over a pile of fabric and ran over and hugged Joshua as he had never been hugged in his life. "How I missed you! I thought I was never goin' to see you again. Where'd you disappear to, man? I been askin' everybody about you."

"I've been around, doing a little P.R. work as you would call it."

"P.R. for what?"

"To prepare people for all the change that is taking place with the new project that's going up."

"Man, that project is humungous. Everybody's talking about it. You mean you're doing P.R. for the project? You really doin' work for a change?"

"Well, not really. But I have a fairly good idea how the project can be a big help to the people, and if they can become interested in it, it can make a big difference in their lives."

In the meantime, the Irishman had just stood there very respectfully listening to the conversation. Elijah had told him all about Joshua, and he was happy just listening to him.

"Oh, by the way, Joshua, this is my friend Kevin. He's from Ireland, but he's a nice man and a good friend. Actually, he started out being Gordon's friend, but I stole him. Kevin's staying with his uncle, who is a good friend of our uncle who you met at church one morning, remember, when you went to Mass."

"Yes, I remember very well. I'll never forget that morning. I was deeply touched by the love and caring those people had for one another."

Kevin and Joshua just looked at each other and nodded recognition. They both knew it was impossible to say anything while Elijah was talking. He didn't even stop to breathe.

Gordon just looked on patiently. He loved his brother. He was dearer to him than anything else in this world. He could see the immense goodness and innocence beneath the bravado and the big mouth. And he knew all the secret deeds of kindness and charity his brother did with his newfound wealth. He was literally picking kids off the streets and putting their lives back together again, and getting some of them to go to good schools, paying the bills himself. He salvaged dozens of young drug dealers who were just getting started, and talked them into going back to school. He spent a lot of his spare time with them, keeping them busy and paying them for little jobs they would do for him. He had almost single-handedly cleaned up the whole little neighborhood around their block. A hard-core pusher would no longer dare come into the local neighborhood. He'd be spotted and turned in immediately.

Other things Gordon knew about his brother impressed him deeply. One night he got up to go to the bathroom and happened to see his brother on his knees in front of the parlor window, praying quietly. He said nothing and silently returned to his room. He knew Elijah had been staying up late but thought nothing of it. It seemed that when Joshua was staying at their house Elijah had woken up and seen Joshua praying like that and was touched by it. So Elijah had been imitating him ever since. It might be hard for others to see much on the surface of Elijah's life, because he fooled around so much, but Gordon looked upon his brother more and more as a saint.

When Elijah finally took time out to breathe, Joshua turned to Kevin and asked about himself and his uncle and his family back home in Ireland.

Out of habit, Kevin started answering Joshua in rap talk. When he realized it, he got embarrassed and spoke straight.

"Joshua," Gordon broke in, "I hope you can wait until we finish so you can come home with us for supper. Mama would love to see you."

"I would enjoy having supper with all of you," Joshua replied.

"Kevin'll be comin' too," Elijah broke in.

"He's sort of family now," Gordon said, complaining. "I can't escape from those two even when I go home."

The brothers showed Joshua around their little

warehouse. It had grown unbelievably in the short time they had been in business. The other workers were happy to finally meet Joshua. They had heard so much about him.

Joshua was impressed at how well they all got along, especially considering the diversity of the group. They had recently hired a Chinese man, a young, wiry fellow with a lively sense of humor, an expert with fabrics, by the name of Moon Wing Hill. His playful humor and ready wit won the hearts of everyone. He had never felt so accepted by Americans as he did when the two black brothers hired him. It was a credit to Gordon and Elijah that they could be so open and objective in their hiring policy. It was actually good business. They hired only the best no matter where they found them. Their customers benefited and it was reflected dramatically in their income reports. Moon Wing got his Chinese friends' business. Kevin got his Irish friends to have their upholstering done there. The same with the others. It would be a full-time job just servicing the orders the employees brought in, and the two brothers made sure they shared generously in the profits. It was teamwork at its best where everyone profited.

Dinner at Josephine's that night was a festive occasion. As more money was coming into the house, Josephine was able to give free rein to all her hidden gourmet talents. Gordon had called her as soon as Joshua appeared at the shop, and she immediately started preparing a feast, so when they all arrived at home, the table was already set and the food was hot in the oven.

"Joshua, Joshua, where have you been? You will never know how we missed you. We thought we would never see you again. And look at the surprise we have waiting for you!

My daughter finally came home after finishing summer school.

"Corinne, this is our friend Joshua we have all been talking about. Isn't he a wonderful man?"

Joshua held both her hands in his and smiled a broad smile. "I was hoping I would get a chance to see you. You sure are the beautiful young lady your mother and brothers say you are. I am very happy to finally meet you."

"I am happy to meet you, Joshua. I hope you don't think evil of me. I didn't run away. I just had to get away if I was going to make anything of myself. I have been going to school and will be going back in another few days. I am very happy with it and just know everything is going to work out. So all Mama's fears are needless. I am doing wonderfully."

It seemed as if Corinne was speaking more to her mother than to Joshua. Joshua just listened and when she finished told her she had made a good decision. After they had sat down for dinner, in no time at all the conversation worked its way to the new project, which was the talk of the whole neighborhood.

"What do you think of the new project?" Corinne asked Joshua.

"I think it will bring about a remarkable change in the lives of everyone living in the area," he answered.

"Do you think it's practical?" she continued.

"You mean, will it work?" he responded.

"Yes."

"It will work as long as people are interested in it working. If they really want to better their lives, this will give everyone an excellent vehicle for improving their lot. It may not be financially practical for the developers in the beginning, but in the long run they will benefit handsomely in ways they never realized."

"They plan on opening up the first phase by late next spring," Elijah said. "They been showin' pictures of the stores and shops they got planned. Gordon and I are thinkin' of movin' into one of them, actually two of them merged together, so we can have a showroom and a large enough size workroom in the back."

"Joshua, I am so proud of my children. They have turned out to be everything I dreamed. For the first time in my life I sleep well. Most of it is thanks to you, Joshua. What a difference you have made in the lives of all of us, and not just ourselves but the whole community."

"You are good people to work with, Josephine, and I am happy everything is flourishing. Your faith and your prayers have been rewarded," Joshua answered. "As I wandered through the neighborhood, I have seen the many good things you have done for others. You and your children have enriched the lives of many, even when you had little yourselves."

The evening passed by quickly, and it was late into the night when they finally retired.

XIV

THE MEETING AT Daniel's office went well. Joshua beamed when he saw the architect's renderings of the project and miniature cardboard models of the buildings. Daniel had even included in the project a small cultural center where people of different ethnic backgrounds living in the neighborhood could hold events and have cultural exhibitions and a host of other programs. Joshua was impressed. An edifice as grand as that in their community would give the people a sense of pride and could even draw visitors from other areas as well as tourists to attend dances and musicales and other programs which, with training, people in the neighborhood could perform themselves. Joshua also added a number of suggestions which Daniel noted. One thing he was very concerned about. He knew the synagogue where his Hasidic friends worshiped would be torn down, as would a mosque in the area. They were small buildings and rather unsightly since the congregations were not wealthy. Joshua asked Daniel if he would have his architects design fitting places of worship to replace the ones they were going to tear down. Daniel was frankly surprised at Joshua's openness and questioned him. Joshua merely said, "Those people worship my Father in the sincerity of their hearts and, even though they do not know Him as I do, they still pray to Him with hearts open to His grace, and deserve a place where they can worship Him with pride and dignity."

Daniel acquiesced.

Joshua also met the young man Daniel was concerned about, and talked with him at length. He could see how deeply involved he was in drugs and knew, like Jeremy, it would be a long time before he was ready to straighten out his life. Joshua promised to pray for him, and asked the boy, whose name was Andrew, to meet with him at certain times to share with him his progress. The young man promised he would.

Although Joshua met with the young man as agreed, no one else was to see Joshua for a long time. Even Daniel's men could not find him. They really did not need him as they had all the important information required to finish the plans. Rumors had it that he had been seen in other neighborhoods around the area but those reports could not be verified. He did visit the campus of the local university and met Harriet, the girl he had encountered on a previous occasion. She repeated her invitation to come and speak with her professor whom she had already told about Joshua. The professor was very interested in meeting with him, so she had promised to make the arrangements if she ever saw Joshua again. When she did by chance meet him walking down the street, she was quite surprised. They talked for a while and, when she asked Joshua about meeting with her teacher, he readily accepted.

The meeting took place the day afterward. Joshua met Harriet around dinnertime at the entrance to the campus and they walked over to the professor's apartment, where they were to have dinner together. The professor was a jolly man, of average height, rather round, with thick white hair and dark brown eyes that twinkled. As soon as Joshua saw him, he liked him and knew they were going to have a happy evening.

"Welcome to my modest home, Joshua! Tom Morrison's my name. I feel I already know you. I can't tell you how happy I am to have this chance to talk with you. Harriet was quite impressed with the conversation she had with you earlier in the summer. She is, and I don't intend to flatter her, my best student. I expect to hear great things about her in the future."

Ushering the two visitors through the apartment, he led them into the living room, which was spacious for a city apartment and had a gorgeous view of the river and the opposite shore. The room was well appointed and in good taste.

"May I offer you some refreshment while we are waiting for our dinner?"

"Yes, I'll have a sherry if you have it, or something light," Joshua replied.

"Sherry it is. I just happen to like it myself, so I keep it in stock."

"Harriet?"

"Just a diet drink of some kind, whatever you have."

"Coming up."

The food cooking on the grill in the kitchen sent an aroma throughout the apartment, making everyone's mouth water.

"I hope you all like steak. I took it upon myself to presume that you might like steak for supper."

"I can tell it is going to be delicious," Joshua answered.

After showing Harriet and Joshua around his home, which he was obviously proud of, the three sat down and plunged into conversation.

"Joshua, would I be rude if I asked about yourself? I am quite curious. Where are you from?"

"I've come from another world really." (Which comment Joshua knew his host would take figuratively.) "I enjoy traveling and I like people, and for the past few months I've been wandering around the local neighborhoods, getting acquainted with the people, listening to them as they tell me about their lives. They are an interesting people, the people who live in this area. They have quite a history and their lives are unfolding in a way that is quite similar to that of the Jewish people of centuries ago when they wandered into the Promised Land. Their lives here have been difficult, but they have a glorious future ahead of them."

"That's an interesting theory!" Tom replied. "Rather fascinating! What do you see them doing in the future that you consider so glorious?"

"They are a warm people and they are a caring people. I see them each day. They have little, but they reach out to one another and share their lives with one another. They have an amazing amount of talent and genius buried within them just waiting to be let loose. When it is, it will explode into a vast cultural revival throughout the country. You can begin to see it already with their music and their dance and their art. As they feel more comfortable about expressing themselves, other aspects of their life will emerge. They have an innately healthy view of life and are not afraid to allow themselves to be open to God. That will one day be the basis for a whole new way of life in the country. The only thing that can threaten that are their leaders. Many of them have sacrificed their cultural heritage for power and prestige and have sold their souls for a pot of porridge. The people should not let shabby leaders with loud and empty voices hoodwink them. They should choose their leaders, not just follow demagogues who make them believe other people are their enemies. There will always be prejudice but, with enthusiasm and determination, these people can rise above others' prejudice to whatever heights they choose, especially in a country like this. Leaders who polarize are their real enemy. They create enemies from people who would like to be friends and thus multiply obstacles. They try to make their own people think they are their heroes, but in reality they are empty windbags who build walls between people rather than generate good will."

"You really like these people, don't you?" Tom responded.

"Yes. I see a lot of good in them that has gone undeveloped, like a treasure that has yet to be mined."

"Joshua, do you have any theories as to the physical differences in racial characteristics?"

"Over long periods of time, climate, environment, and diet, which is really chemical, can have profound effects on the human body, and can ultimately affect genetic structure. You see this in your own research, how chemicals and radiation can rearrange genetic material and cause mutations. Occurring spontaneously in nature, it usually strengthens the human system as it is forced to adjust to manifold stresses over thousands of years."

"You don't think, then, that all the races had different origins?" Tom continued.

"Not at all. The racial differences are not that great, and are merely physical and superficial, and do not affect the ability of the individuals of different races to marry and have offspring who can themselves have children."

Tom was impressed with Joshua's answers, as Harriet had already told him that Joshua had no real formal education, especially on the level that would give him an understanding of genetics.

"Harriet told me about some of your ideas on genetic engineering. I am very curious to hear about them," Tom hinted. "There are so many conflicting attitudes. Some think they are a great and beneficial breakthrough. Others think they are totally immoral and tampering with God's creation. Other attitudes are quite bizarre and frightening. How do you feel about it, Joshua?"

"First of all, life is sacred, especially human life. It mirrors God, and each individual is a unique creation destined to perform a certain necessary work. From the first spark of its existence it is sacred, and must be treasured, like the discovery of a rare seed of an extinct plant that flourished a half million years ago and now, having been recently found, is capable of resurrecting that species once again. The uniqueness of that seed is nothing compared to the uniqueness of a human. Each human being is not just another human being that is replicable and therefore disposable. It is a unique creation and will never again be replaced, nor will its function be replaceable. So, starting from that principle, you go further.

"While God created humans perfectly in the beginning, natural factors and artificial factors have caused breakdowns in the human genetic material which have caused severe damage to the health and well-being of God's children. That is unfortunate, but God gave intelligence to human beings and intended they should use that intelligence to perfect what has been accidentally damaged. God has always worked in partnership with His human creatures and inspires them to find solutions to problems in nature. It is a good and noble work to correct the damage done to the human person, whether that damage be physical, emotional, mental, or spiritual. That work must always be done with awe in the realization that that life belongs to God. We are not the creators of our own existence. When a geneticist keeps that in mind, he or she can be proud to be sharing in God's own power to create. How much closer can a person be to God than when the two work together in the most intimate way in perfecting the very blueprints of life itself."

"That's a mouthful, Joshua," Harriet said, finally breaking her silence.

"It is beautiful, Joshua," Tom added. "I have never heard it expressed that way before. It elevates a scientist from a mere technician to a level that is really noble and awesome."

"If people only knew how special they are. You don't have to be a scientist to be special. Each individual has been created to touch the lives of certain other people and affect the whole course of their existence. Everyone depends on others for what is lacking in each. That is the way my Father designed His creation."

While Joshua was talking Tom panicked. The odor of steak burning was floating into the living room.

"Whew," Tom aspirated as he mopped his face with his handkerchief. "I thought they had burned, but they are just nicely charred. Why don't we all come into the dining room and sit down and enjoy our meal?"

Harriet told Joshua on the way to the dining room how happy she was over what he had said. It all made such good sense. She had sort of felt that way but had not put it all together in her mind in a way that seemed logical and orderly.

The remainder of the evening went well. The three

ended up becoming good friends and decided to keep in touch with one another if at all possible. Harriet and Tom were baffled when they asked Joshua for his address and phone number and he told them he did not live in any particular place and of course had no phone. Tom immediately told him he was more than welcome to stay at his place any time he had no place to sleep or when the weather was bad. Joshua thanked him and said he might take him up on his offer if the occasion ever arose.

Other than that meeting and his occasional sessions with Andrew, Joshua's presence in the neighborhood was seen but rarely.

The months went by fast. All his friends missed him, particularly Daniel, who was always eager to share the progress reports with him. Much was actually done on the project while Joshua was away. The first phase of the construction was pretty well finished by spring. As Daniel wanted to get the project finished as soon as possible, crews were working on all phases of the project at the same time, so what would have taken many years was pretty well telescoped into a much shorter time.

When Joshua did finally put in an appearance it was well into spring. Construction of most of the buildings was well on its way. The shell of the cultural center was finished and turned out to be a gorgeous piece of architecture. Many of the houses were almost ready for occupancy. The neighborhood schools were completed. A number of the mini-factories were almost ready for use. The shops where Gordon and Elijah were relocating were ready and, as the two brothers had already signed leases with Daniel's agents, they would move in at the first possible chance.

When Daniel met Joshua at the site, he was surprised but said nothing. He was just glad to see him. They hugged. Joshua noticed Daniel had tears in his eyes when he met him. The first thing he mentioned to Joshua was Andrew.

"Joshua, I don't know what you did to that boy. He's a changed person. I had been so concerned about him. He's been off drugs for months now and is back to his happy, bright self. His work is extraordinary. Much of the engineering work on the project he did by himself and his work is impeccable. He insisted on doing the engineering work for the synagogue and the mosque because he knew they were special to you and he did a marvelous job on them. We can drive over later on and see the progress, though they won't be finished for another month or so."

"Daniel, I am very impressed with what you have accomplished. It is truly an amazing feat that you have been able to assign your people to work on all phases of the project simultaneously."

"I really had to finish this operation in record time, so I can get back to my other work and make money to pay for this one. It is still going to take a good while before everything is fully completed. But, hopefully, by next year we should have the last of the buildings complete and the finishing work done on everything. One of the nice things I have learned on this project is how enthusiastically the neighborhood people are working. They hardly ever miss a day. I'm thinking seriously about hiring a good number of them to work permanently for the company. They have been very loyal and earn every cent of what I pay them."

Daniel and Joshua had lunch together, talked over personal things, one of which was Charlene's progress. Daniel and Jana were proud of her. She had done well her first year at boarding school. They had spent a very happy Christmas together and hoped Joshua would show up, which would have made it complete. Charlene would be coming home shortly and Daniel hoped Joshua would stop over for a visit, which he promised he would do. After lunch the two men separated, Daniel going back to work and Joshua wandering into another nearby neighborhood.

This neighborhood was on the perimeter of the development. The ethnic mix was different than the ones next to it, having a sprinkling of Arab-speaking people from Lebanon, Syria, Iran, and Afghanistan. Though some were Christians, most were Muslims, many of whom had been attending the mosque that had been torn down to make way for the development project.

Joshua fitted well into this assortment of people. It was easy for him to switch from Hebrew to Arabic, thereby impressing whomever he talked to. One was a Lebanese trader who owned an antique store. Walking along the street, Joshua noticed an icon of his Mother in the window. It impressed him deeply because it was the only picture of his Mother he had ever seen which really looked like her. It was an old icon, perhaps two hundred years old, and framed in beautifully hammered silver. Joshua was moved by it and went into the store to ask the owner how much he wanted for it.

"Eighteen hundred dollars but, for you, I can tell you are a discriminating man with good taste, I will sell it to you for sixteen hundred."

Joshua was disappointed.

"If I paid a small amount each week for the next four months, could I have it?"

"Sorry, I don't do business like that. Do you have a credit card?"

"Credit card? No, I'm afraid I don't have anything like that."

"Why do you like the icon so much?" the owner asked Joshua.

"Because it looks so much like my Mother."

"Well, I'll take another fifty dollars off for that."

"Thank you, but that won't change my financial situation."

"Why don't you just take a photograph of your mother?"

"That would really be difficult."

"How come?"

"She's in heaven."

"That icon is not a painting of an ordinary person, you know. That's the Mother of God."

"I know. It's a good representation."

Getting impatient at the realization he was wasting his time, the owner told Joshua to come back when he got the money and he would be glad to sell it to him.

"I'm very busy and I can't spend any more time with you. I'm sure it won't sell immediately. So, when you get the money, come back and it's yours. Have a good day!"

"You also," Joshua said as he looked sentimentally at the icon and walked out of the shop, disappointed.

Joshua had been hoping he could buy the painting and give it as a present to Daniel and Jana and Charlene. It would be a most beautiful gift, knowing that his very dear friends would have a rare picture of his Mother that looked just like her.

"It's not easy being poor," Joshua reflected. "Though money is the cheapest thing on earth, it is, unfortunately, the means to the fulfillment of so many dreams, good dreams. People who have been blessed with much must help others who have little to find the means to attain their dreams. Not caring about the shattered dreams of others is a horrible sin when my Father has given some people so much and they hoard it for themselves. People don't realize that, when they are called to answer for their use of my Father's gifts to them, He is not going to ask them how much they made, but how much they gave away, how they channeled His goodness into the lives of others in need."

As Joshua walked up the street, three men attacked him from behind. Fortunately, he sensed they were approaching him and turned immediately to protect himself. Four strangers walking down the other side of the street saw what was happening. They ran across the street and pulled the three men off Joshua and scuffled with them till the three realized they were outmatched and ran off.

The four men lifted him from the sidewalk and brushed the dust from his clothes. Joshua thanked them profusely, and the men replied in Arabic, which Joshua picked up on and spoke to them in their native tongue. They were delighted and stayed to talk with him for quite a while, fascinated by all that Joshua had to tell them. The men told Joshua all about themselves and where they had grown up, and how they had only recently come to this country. They invited Joshua to stop at a Turkish restaurant and have a cup of Turkish coffee with them. Joshua was delighted with their friendliness.

Once seated in the restaurant, the men introduced themselves: Ali Bashir, Malek Bennabi, Mohammed Said, and Jakob al-Wahdi. Although the men came from different countries, they had met one another when they came to worship at the local mosque and had become good friends.

"Yes," Ali told Joshua, "we used to pray together at the mosque, but they tore it down for the new development."

"It turned out to be a blessing in disguise because the developer must be a nice man. He asked a few of our leaders if we would meet with his architects so they could build a new mosque for us. It is almost finished and is going to be beautiful. Would you like to come and see it when it is finished? In fact, you might like to come to the dedication."

"I would be thrilled," Joshua told the men.

As the men were not sure of the date, Joshua assured them he would have no trouble finding out and would meet them there on that happy occasion.

"You come as our guest and feast with us after the dedication ceremony," Jakob added.

"Thank you, thank you all so much," Joshua said to them. "You are fine gentlemen, and I know Allah is pleased with you."

"You are Muslim?" Ali asked.

"No. We all worship the One God. We just call Him by different names," Joshua responded.

Finishing their coffee, the men rose and left the restaurant, taking leave of their new friend and promising to see him on the dedication day.

Walking along the street, Joshua realized he was in a

different kind of neighborhood. The farther south he walked the more different it became. There was a loneliness, a coldness that made him feel uncomfortable. Too many people of too many different ethnic backgrounds, all shunning one another, building invisible barriers and avoiding even looking at one another on the streets, so as not to make a contact that might in some way lead to even a minimum of intimacy, or even friendliness.

He finally approached a hospital rising imposingly on the opposite side of the street. He decided to stop and casually visit the patients.

Hard-pressed nurses were running everywhere, trying desperately to finish their daily routine. Some seemed aggressively efficient but lacked compassion. For some, each patient seemed almost like a family member. He quietly smiled a hello to them. One lady he visited had been there for over three months. No one knew what to do for her. She had had a stroke, but with the therapy she was almost totally recuperated but could not go home because there was no one to care for her. Her family never visited her and she was slowly dying from loneliness. As Joshua walked past her room, he looked in and saw her and, in that simple glance, saw her whole life and all her anguish. He stopped.

"Hello, my name is Joshua. What is your name?"

"Agnes."

"That's a beautiful name. You even look like a gentle lamb."

They talked for a while. The woman ended up telling him she wished she could go home, but her children didn't even visit her and there would be no one to take care of her. Most of her old friends had moved to better neighborhoods. She had decided to stay behind, and now she had few friends except for some elderly black people who had been wonderful to her. "But they have their own problems and heartaches, and I can't expect them to come in to check on me all day long."

Joshua could see her desperate loneliness and the results of her debilitating stroke which had effectively imprisoned her within herself.

"Agnes, what would you do if you were freed of your illness and could run around again?" Joshua asked her.

"If I had the use of my limbs, I have already made up my mind what I would do. I can see how many there are here who are just dumped here by family and no one ever comes to visit them. Since all my friends are gone and my family has no time for me, I'll be darned if I'd just lock myself in the house and feel sorry for myself. I think I'd spend most of my time visiting people in the hospitals and nursing homes, and let them know that there is someone who loves them and cares for them. I would help them to realize they are never alone. Jesus is always by their side, and I'd leave them a picture of Him, a nice picture, not one of those soupy, sentimental ones. In fact, you'd make a good model for a picture of Jesus. Why don't you pose for one?"

Joshua laughed. "They might find me unacceptable."

"True, you don't have a beard and Jesus has a beard."

"See what I mean? Agnes, you are a beautiful soul. My Father still has work for you to do, so do not be discouraged. You have many lives to touch and many hearts to heal. When you go home tomorrow, don't be afraid, you will be able to take care of yourself, and you will have all you need to keep your independence. So don't be afraid."

Saying this, he placed his hand on her head and merely said, "Agnes, be well so you can go out and serve the Lord."

Not understanding it all, but realizing something wonderful had happened inside, the woman began to cry and the tears flowed down her cheeks in torrents.

"Thank you, Joshua. Thank you so much. I will never forget you, whoever you are."

She took his hand and kissed it tenderly. Then Joshua left.

Taking the elevator to another floor, he arrived at the ward which housed the AIDS patients. The first room he entered had only one patient. A friend was sitting by the patient's bedside. Joshua asked if he could come in. They both eyed him with suspicion.

The man lying in the bed was all but drained of life, nothing more than a skeleton with a thin layer of skin drawn taut to hide the bones. Walking close to the bed, Joshua could see the agony reflected in the dying man's eyes. He had endured a thousand purgatories. He could see the desolation, the loneliness, the fear of dying, of meeting God, wondering if God even wanted him when no one else did, the pain of leaving someone who had given him friendship and love, when even family would have nothing to do with him.

Seeing all the pain as only Joshua could, his heart almost broke and tears welled up in his eyes.

"Peace, Timothy, be at peace. Your soul is pure, cleansed and purified by the pain and anguish you have suffered so patiently. The many good deeds you have done for others, especially your kindness to the homeless and the lonely, have touched my Father's heart. Redeemed by His Son's death, you are precious. So do not be afraid! When you close your eyes this evening, you will open them in paradise. Be at peace. There is nothing to fear. God will take care of your companion. He has been loyal to you and his love for you has been generous and unselfish. God will protect him, and you will see him again."

"You are a strange man. How do you know me? Who are you?" the dying man asked in disbelief.

"I am whom your heart tells you I am."

At those words, the young man began to cry and, taking Joshua's hand, kissed it; through his tears and weakened voice, he looked into Joshua's eyes and said, "Thank you. Now I will die in peace."

Joshua bent over and kissed him on the forehead and, placing his hand on his head, blessed him and his companion, then walked out.

It had been a strenuous day and Joshua was tired. He walked back toward the construction site. As it was evening he found a small clump of trees behind the site where he could sleep for the night. It was a little oasis of peace and quiet where he could rest undisturbed and get a good night's sleep. Falling on his knees and sitting back on his heels, he placed his hands in his lap and prayed silently for the longest time, then fell down upon the ground totally exhausted and went into a sound sleep.

Hardly had he closed his eyes when a blinding light woke him. "Get up out of there, you bum!" a voice out of the darkness shouted at him. It was a security guard patrolling the construction site.

Joshua rubbed his eyes, said nothing, realizing it would accomplish nothing, and walked away into the darkness.

"This is how they treat the poor and the homeless. It hurts. It strips one of pride and dignity," Joshua thought.

He walked through the streets toward the waterfront. He knew it was not safe there, but where to go? "It must be a frightening thing to have to live this way every day and every night," he reflected.

Walking toward the river, where there was at least a cool breeze coming in off the water, he sat down and rested his weary body against a stanchion. Before he even had a chance to close his eyes, he noticed a huge animal approaching. As it came closer, he could see it looked like a dog, but much larger. He was shocked for a moment when he realized it was a wolf, a real wolf in the middle of the city.

The animal came over to him, paused for a few seconds and sniffed at Joshua's feet, then walked alongside him and began to lick his hand. Joshua petted the huge animal and talked to him. Without any more to-do, the wolf lay down next to Joshua and fell asleep. A few times during the night strangers approached in the dark, but immediately panicked and took off when the huge animal growled at them.

Next morning at sunrise, Joshua and the wolf awoke.

"You've been a good friend. Protected me all night, didn't you?" he said to the animal as he petted him on the head.

Noticing a collar and license around his neck, Joshua stooped to read it. "My name is Peter. I belong to Craig." Then the address and phone number.

Joshua walked toward the city and began another day. He would find Craig somehow or other.

XV

AT FIRST, NEWSPAPERS ignored Daniel's project.
People, from government officials to people in the streets,
were weary of the never-ending building projects. So the
news media deemed this project just another of the endless
nuisances and passed it over as unnewsworthy. However, the
dimensions of this undertaking were of such gigantic
proportions, it could not be ignored for long. The reality of
its vastness struck with all its stunning impact as every phase
of the undertaking began to emerge simultaneously from the
ruins of the old neighborhood, like some monstrous creature
rising out of the flattened, desolate earth almost overnight.
The project covered an area of over eight hundred acres, if
you included the mini-parks and neighborhood playgrounds.
Not a day passed that television crews were not wandering
throughout the site, documenting every facet of the project,
interviewing engineers, architects, workmen, and even the
laborers, attempting to cover the stories from every possible
angle. Reporters were surprised to learn that the vast
majority of the workers were from the neighborhood itself.
What a novel approach to urban renewal!

Associated Press reporters George Cornell and Ron
Lesco came on different occasions. George, to study the
ecumenical implications of various aspects of the
development; Ron, to research the sports and cultural
aspects of the project. Their articles brought national
attention to the project, and before long politicians from
around the country were crawling all over the place, much to

Daniel's annoyance as they were distracting him from overseeing the details of the construction, about which he was meticulous.

Everyone was impressed. The concepts were so new and so simple, people wondered why no one had thought of them before. The important thing was that they were practical and workable. Work *should* be available near where people live. Schools *should* cater to the needs of the students and not to the political needs of the school officials. Every child will not go to college. They can still be geniuses whose talents *must* be developed for their benefit as well as for the benefit of society and the industries that will employ them. Parents and industry *should* have a controlling voice in the running of the schools. It is a natural and healthy partnership. In compacted areas children should not have to make playgrounds out of the streets. Playgrounds *should* be part of every neighborhood. People in neighborhoods, whether they are young or old, need recreation. They shouldn't have to spend half of a week's income to have a night out or few hours' recreation. Neighborhood centers, whatever they might be called, *should* be a part of every community so the people can gather for dances and recreation and community meetings, and whatever other cultural programs they may be interested in. Churches used to fill those functions, but no more, which is better because they isolated people from others in the community. This way they all can work together in a more open and unifying spirit.

The park on the river with a community-operated marina and restaurant really piqued the interest of the reporters. They had not come across such an idea before. Even people of modest means could use the marina and rent boats for a jaunt on the river and a reasonably priced dinner at the restaurant afterward.

No more high-rise "prisons" that only drove people to the fringes of insanity, and whose only escape was a black-topped park where grown-ups could sit and stare into space or watch kids bouncing basketballs off noisy backdrops twenty-four hours a day.

The cultural center was Jana's dream. The reporters had a difficult time tracking her down, as she was constantly on the move. She took a personal interest in the construction of the center, so she spent most of her time there, watching over every detail. When they finally found her, she explained everything to their complete delight. That in itself was a good human interest story. There would be classrooms where children could learn music and dancing and acting and painting and other forms of art. She would subsidize the hiring of teachers for the programs and also help with expenses for putting on plays or musicals or art exhibitions. And she would insist that everything be done with real class so they could attract visitors from other cities to come and enjoy the fruit of the neighborhood talent.

The reporters were also curious about the small factories being built. The products manufactured would run the gamut of modern discoveries from simple electronic items to highly technical products, and even though only components might be manufactured locally, they would still be necessary industries that would provide job stability to the neighborhood. The buildings under construction for these operations were themselves neat, contemporary structures that would give real class to the neighborhood.

Since there would also be parks and playgrounds scattered throughout the development, neighborhood people were already being trained to do the landscaping and caretaking once they were laid out and ready for planting. This fascinated the reporters because they could see the hope this project gave to everyone who before had just been given shelter but no one really cared for them or saw much value in them. Now they had hope, the quality of the work was much above average because it was to be their neighborhood and it could stand up to any part of the city no matter how classy. People had a chance to rise above themselves and this they did with dignity and style. The reporters were impressed. With care and appreciation of people's worth, it could be done. It was being done. A model for others to imitate if they so chose.

During all this time Joshua kept a low profile. The last thing he wanted was publicity. His ideas moved under their own momentum. His identity was not important. Though he was not seen often, mention was made of individuals encountering him at times, like Craig, the wolf's owner, who met Joshua one day when the animal led him to his master, and his meeting with Georgeanne's little family, who still depended on him for guidance and support, and the time when Elijah decided to throw a party for Joshua and had his friends comb the neighborhood until they found him. The two brothers always felt sorry for Joshua because he had no money. But he would never take anything, saying he really did not need it. This time, however, was different. The party was held at the upholstery shop. It was just a simple party, an excuse to give Joshua a gift. A number of his friends were invited. They just had a simple lunch together and told Joshua how much they appreciated all that he had done for them and that no matter what happened they would never forget him. Then they presented him with an envelope with a very touching card inside. Also tucked inside were sixteen one-hundred-dollar bills.

Joshua opened the card and read it, and saw the bills. Tears welled up in his eyes. He looked around at each one and just said, "Thank you. I too will never forget you. You are all very special to me and always will be. Thank you for your friendship."

Needless to say, after the party Joshua made a beeline for the antique shop, to buy the picture of his Mother, which he asked the owner to wrap for him. As he had to figure out how to present the gift to Daniel and Jana and Charlene, he called them and invited himself over for dinner that night. Of course, they were thrilled that he felt close enough to them to just call and say he was coming over.

It was while sitting in the living room before supper that he presented them with the icon.

"The three of you have been such good friends, and have shown such boundless generosity to so many people, I wanted to give you a token of my appreciation and my friendship."

Then he presented them with the icon. When they opened the package, they were awed by the beauty of it.

"Joshua, it is beautiful!" Jana said. "I have never seen such a gorgeous icon. And it is authentic. That must have cost a fortune. I have an icon of Jesus, the Pantocrator, but I always wanted one of His Mother. I could never find one with a happy face. This one is a treasure. Why did you pick this one?"

"Because it looks just like my Mother," he said simply.

There was silence for a moment, then Jana remarked, "She must have been beautiful."

"She is," he answered, then turned to Daniel and told

him about his meeting with the Arab men and how excited they were about their new mosque. Daniel was pleased.

That evening was the last anyone saw of Joshua for a long time. By now everyone was used to his disappearing for extended periods of time and thought nothing of it. It was, however, many months before he returned this time. Many things had changed.

Gordon and Elijah had moved into their new quarters in the new shopping center. A great many of the buildings in the project were finished and inhabited. Stores were open. The schools were open. Factories were moving in equipment to prepare for full operation as soon as the workers were trained. People were busy doing the landscaping throughout the whole development. Water had filled the small lakes in the mini-parks scattered throughout the development. The cultural center was finished and already in use. Jana was spending a good part of her time there, making sure it was being put to full use. And it was.

Walking through the development, Joshua beamed his joy and thrill at what Daniel had accomplished.

"I have never met a man with his goodness and generosity," Joshua reflected. "Would to God there were more like him responding to God's grace! When people open their hearts to God and allow Him to be their partner, and His genius to flow through them, the most wonderful dreams can become reality. And what a beautiful example this is!" Standing on a tiny knoll, his eyes scanned the magnificent panorama as far as he could see. It was breathtaking, awesome. He was pleased.

XVI

FINISHING TOUCHES ON the construction would go on for at least another year, though most of the buildings were already in use. Joshua enjoyed walking through the newly opened stores. Neighborhood people had been trained to run them. Daniel made sure that only those banks that would lend to the poor would be allowed to open in the development. Once the people proved they could run their little businesses, financing was arranged for them to own the businesses. A team of consultants was permanently available to help anyone with problems. Their fees were modest.

Most of the businesses were doing quite well and, with help, those faltering were able to improve, though it would take time. Gordon and Elijah's upholstery business was booming. They were well established now and, with people in the area earning good salaries, prettying up their homes was high on their priority list.

The house Josephine and her family moved into was a large home, with four bedrooms, a sunken living room, and something Josephine had dreamed of all her life: a large kitchen with a counter in the center and a butler's pantry attached. They started a garden for the first time in their lives and were having so much fun caring for it. The family had never been happier.

A few months after the development was finished, Gordon and Elijah heard rumors of a competitor opening not too far from them, just outside the development. At first they paid no attention, then they became concerned when they found out that the prices their competitor was charging were far below anything they could charge and survive. The new place was a big operation and obviously heavily capitalized to lose money on such low prices. It was obviously a calculated risk. They knew the brothers had been in business only a couple of years and could not long survive a price war. They were willing to lose considerable money for a few months until they drove Gordon and Elijah out of business.

Elijah could not wait to tell Joshua and ask what they should do. Joshua just laughed.

"Don't worry," he said.

" 'Don't worry,' he says," Elijah retorted, "when we're about to lose our shirts, and our pants as well, and everything else besides."

"When you do good, God always takes care of you," Joshua reassured him and Gordon.

"But we need money, man, and God don't give out no money," Elijah continued.

"Just watch and see what happens. You'll be pleasantly surprised," Joshua told them.

"I hope so. I sure hope so," Gordon replied, finally breaking his silence.

That night Joshua had a meeting with Daniel and told him of the situation. Always the businessman, Daniel pumped Joshua with questions.

"What kind of businessmen are the two brothers? Do they have a going business?" he asked.

"They are excellent businessmen. I trained them myself."

"Hmmm. That's an interesting recommendation!"

"And their business?"

"Daniel, they started out with nothing hardly two and a half years ago and, with careful planning, built up the business to what it is today without ever borrowing a penny from the banks. You can feel very secure with them."

"Well, what do you think we should do, since we are really partners in this whole operation?"

"Why not subsidize their business for a while, so they can lower their prices beyond the competition until they can drive them out of business?"

"Joshua, you're tough! I never saw that trait in you before."

"I have a hard time with mean people. There is no reason those people couldn't have just opened their business. They would have done well. There is more than enough business for both of them. But we are dealing with greedy people and they want it all for themselves. Now they'll see what they are up against."

"All right, tell the brothers to go ahead and lower their prices. But don't let them know who's subsidizing them. They can pay me back when it's all over. In fact, I have a better idea. I have some furniture that has to be done over. I'll arrange for them to do it and pay them beforehand. That way they will have all the cash they need. But they had better give me a darn good price on this job."

Joshua laughed and, as he thanked Daniel and was about to leave, Daniel said to him, "You're not getting away that easy. This is going to cost you. We'll be expecting you at the house tonight for supper."

"That's a high price to pay, but . . . I'll be there," he said, smiling, and walked out.

The next day Gordon was called down to Daniel's office and asked for an on-the-spot estimate for redoing furniture in a number of Daniel's offices. Gordon was dumbfounded at the size of the order and sensed Joshua was behind it somehow, but couldn't imagine Joshua's connection with Daniel Trumbull. He figured he had better give a good discount on this one.

Daniel was pleased with the estimate and had his treasurer cut the check immediately and give it to Gordon. He was wide-eyed, and thanked the man profusely, and said he would send a truck over that afternoon to pick up the furniture.

When Joshua stopped in the store that afternoon, Gordon could not wait to tell him, and then asked him what he should do with the check.

"Bank it immediately of course, and take out an ad in the paper announcing a dramatic reduction in prices."

"Dramatic."

"Yes, you don't want to waste time. Get this thing done and over with, and get back to your work."

"Joshua, you frighten me. You can be as cold as ice when you have a mind to."

"Only toward those who are mean and vicious."

"Joshua, you teach forgiveness. Don't you think we should go over and talk to those people first?" Elijah asked.

"Elijah, you have a kind heart. But I know what's in people's hearts, and those people are hard and callous. They would just laugh at you and say, 'Sorry, but that's business. If you can't stand the heat, then get out of the kitchen.' I know that kind. They have no heart."

"Joshua, you amaze me."

"Let's stop talking. Bank the check and let's get going."

The war went on for almost three weeks. Then, one day, a customer came into the store and told Gordon and Elijah there was a sign on their competitor's window. "Close Out Sale. Store will be closing at the end of the week." They all rejoiced. Everybody in the shop started dancing for sheer joy. They had won. They had won, in fair competition. Their first big battle. And they were smart enough to make sure their competition was really closing before they raised their prices, which they did only gradually, being careful to explain to their customers that they had taken great losses during the price war.

When Joshua showed up a few days later, they couldn't wait to tell him. He, too, was happy. Joshua told them to make sure they did a good job on Mr. Trumbull's furniture and did not keep him waiting too long.

With the phenomenal growth of their upholstery business, the two brothers set up a fund to help others. They were subsidizing needy students' education, funding scholarships at Jana's cultural center, helping others get started in business, and answering a host of other needs in the community. It seemed the more generous they were in helping others the faster their business grew.

"My Father will not be outdone in generosity," Joshua told the brothers one day.

With all the wonderful things happening in the community, it seemed as if the messianic age had arrived. Everything seemed more like a dream than reality. But the dream did not last for long. Tragedy struck one night when Gordon and Elijah were walking down the street. They had just finished supper and were on their way to a movie. They had met a few of their old friends and were all walking down the street laughing and joking and having a good time, when a car drove past and a shot rang out. Elijah clutched his chest and fell to the sidewalk. Gordon looked toward the car and got a brief glimpse of the fellow with the pistol, a local punk who had been bad news for years.

As the car sped past, Gordon turned around and saw his brother lying on the ground and screamed.

"Eddie, Eddie, what have they done to you?"

Kneeling down, he lifted his brother's head and rested it in his lap, and tried to comfort him. He could see his brother had been shot either in the heart or near it. While one of the men ran to call an ambulance, Gordon bent over and tried to talk to his brother.

"Gordon, don't worry about me. I know I'm going to die. But . . . that's okay. You've been a . . . good . . . brother . . . the best. I love . . . love Mama . . . Corinne . . . Josh . . . ua. I see . . . heaven. Bye . . . dear brother . . . Love you."

"Bye, Eddie. I love you too."

Elijah's chest heaved, then sank. His breathing stopped. Gordon screamed and cried like a baby, unashamedly. People heard it all the way down the street. He pressed his brother's head to his chest and caressed it tenderly.

"This crazy, insane city! What has happened to us? The only innocent soul I ever knew in my whole life, so full of goodness, so full of fun and so gentle, and killed by a damned insane idiot. Will it never end? How can I possibly break the news to Mama? Oh, poor Mama. I know this will kill her. How can I possibly tell her? Yet she has to be told. Oh, God, help me! Bring my brother home! Joshua, where are you? You could have stopped this. You could have saved my brother, if only you were here."

The ambulance arrived, but there was nothing the medics could do. The police also arrived, and asked all kinds of questions. After the police marked the place of the body, the medics took the body to the hospital. Gordon had given them all the information they needed, so he left and went home to break the news to his mother and sister and take them to the hospital.

When he arrived, Joshua was already there talking to Josephine and Corinne.

"How did he know about it?" Gordon thought.

"Elijah was a very special young man," Joshua was telling Josephine and Corinne. "His goodness has touched and changed the lives of countless young people in the neighborhood. His memory will never be forgotten."

"But why, why? He was so good," Josephine sobbed.

"Josephine, it is precisely because he was so good that my Father took him home. I see clearly what his life would have been like if he had lived longer. His sensitive soul could not have endured the betrayals, the cruelty, and the meanness of people, especially of those he would have trusted. It would have crushed his spirit. My Father spared him all that. And besides that, he had a very special work to accomplish and a special message to preach through the goodness of his life. He accomplished that job nobly. There was no more need for him to stay here, so, being very practical, my Father took him home. He is already in heaven. He sees you. He hears us. He is healed and he is smiling. And he is telling you, 'Mama, don't worry about me. I'm happy here. I just saw Grandma. Mama, I'd like to tell you a big secret. You know who's talking to you right now? Mama, if you only knew! Don't worry about me, Mama. I'm home. And I still love you all, you too, Corinne. I'll pester God to take good care of you. He's beautiful, Mama.' "

"Joshua," Josephine cried, "I'm going to miss him so. He was such a pure and innocent boy. No evil in him. How

I'll miss my Elijah! But your words are so comforting. To know he's in heaven is such a reassurance. No more pain, no more hurt, no more problems. God is good. He knows what He is doing. Dear Lord, take good care of my son!"

"Mama, we had better go to the hospital," Gordon said. "They will want to ask us all kinds of questions and to fill out papers."

Joshua embraced each one and prayed for them, asking his Father to send His Spirit and bring them peace. Gordon walked him to the door and, outside, Joshua turned to him and said quietly, "Gordon, forgive, and do not do what is in your heart. It will destroy yourself and your whole family. Just tell the police and let them take care of it."

"Joshua, who are you? How do you know what is in my heart?"

Joshua hugged him. Gordon promised to call the police.

Turning, Joshua left and walked out into the city, tears flowing down his cheeks, praying for the family he loved so much.

XVII

THE FUNERAL WAS held at the Resurrection Baptist Church. Joshua was there, and the minister, knowing how much he meant to the brothers and, indeed, to the whole family, asked if he would sit up front with him and say a few words at the proper time. Joshua said he would be happy to.

The service was filled with pathos. The whole neighborhood had loved Elijah. He radiated fun and laughter and was always kind. There were black people, white people, Chinese people, Spanish people, Catholics, Protestants, Muslims. The whole community was represented. As the crowd was so large, people were standing outside the church as well. A Spanish girl named Carmen sang his favorite hymn, "Goin' Home," from Dvořák's *New World* Symphony. Even though it was not really a hymn, the spiritual connotation was obvious. Elijah had always had the feeling he was going home early and, strangely enough, was not unhappy about it. He and Carmen had always been the best of friends. He had told Carmen he wanted her to sing that song at his funeral. She never dreamed that she would one day have to do it.

The minister tried to give a sermon but broke down. Elijah had been helping the minister and his family secretly, and the man loved him so much for his kindness and generosity that he could not get himself to believe the boy was dead. The man turned toward Joshua and asked if he would speak.

Joshua looked out of place, dressed in his simple clothes,

when everyone else was so properly dressed for a funeral. Some who did not know him were shocked until they heard him speak.

"My friends," Joshua started, "Elijah's laughter still rings in our ears. The last time I heard him speak, he had a thick Irish brogue. Beneath his playfulness and simplicity was a soul as innocent and pure as an angel. In all this great city there is not one as holy, as innocent, and as great as this young man, Elijah. The heart of each one of us is broken by his passing. The streets will hear less laughter, the children will have one less hero, the lonely and the needy will miss his kindness, the whole neighborhood will miss his playfulness now that he is gone. Josephine and Gordon and Corinne will miss him most of all. But they can boast they have a brother who is a saint. Hopefully, God will raise up others to fill the void in the community and again make the streets ring with laughter and fun.

"But we have his memories, and they are many, and they are beautiful. It is a rare person who has not benefited from his kindness and generosity. He was truly God's presence in this community, doing magnificently what each of us should be doing: being the heart and the hands of God to those around us who are hurting.

"Do not weep for Elijah! He is home, as Carmen sang so movingly. He *is* home. He sees God face to face right now, and he is still being the clown in heaven as he was on earth and making everyone laugh. And having seen the beauty and wonder of my Father, nothing could ever draw him back to earth. So do not weep for him. He is at peace, and he is happy. And he watches over all of you with the same tenderness he had when he was with you. God allowed that beautiful young man to be with you for a little while.

Treasure the memory, and may his goodness be ever an inspiration to all of you to love and care for one another the way he did for all of you."

There was not a dry eye in the church when Joshua finished. In fact, they all stood up and clapped and sang "Amen, Alleluia," for almost five minutes after Joshua finished. The rest of the service was lighthearted and filled with real Christian joy, assured now that their dear friend was having fun in heaven.

Toward the end of the service the famous Boys' Choir from the area just north of there sang some of Elijah's favorites. There was a special one called "Joshua's Song" that Elijah had had a friend named Rick compose for him. The choir sang this song. It was a song of peace and forgiveness. After the first verse the whole congregation joined in. It was a stirring finish to a beautiful life.

After the service Carmen approached Joshua and asked if he would visit her church. It was a Spanish parish and they were having a festival in two weeks. She would love for him to come so he could see all that they had accomplished. It was in the area just above this section of the city. The name of her parish was St. Simon-in-the-Tree-Trunk.

"What a strange name!" Joshua said.

"Yes, but it's a wonderful parish. We are all Spanish and black and we are a big caring family. We have the highest percentage of students going to college from our school of any other school in the whole city. There was a big article in the paper about it."

"Carmen, you are so enthusiastic about it. It must be a wonderful community. I would be happy to come."

"And I am going to dance. And I will dance just for you, if you come."

"I'll be there."

Joshua spent the rest of the day alone with his thoughts, just sitting by the river and watching the water flow by. He was sad. Strange. He knew Elijah was in heaven and happy, but he still missed the playfulness and the laughter and, like all the others in the neighborhood, felt deeply the void his friend's passing left in his heart.

Back to reality the next day, Joshua was contacted by Daniel, who wanted to speak with him. It was urgent. The courier drove Joshua to Daniel's office.

"Joshua, please sit down. I have something very important to discuss with you, and I hope you will hear me out," Daniel told him.

"I will listen. Tell me!"

"I received a phone call yesterday from our senator, Senator Moynihan. He and the other congresspeople who were wandering through the development a while back were apparently impressed and have been receiving comments from all across the country about what has happened here. The rest of the Congress wants to know all the details about the project and its progress and how it is working out, and whether we are pleased with the results. They asked if I would come to Washington and speak to Congress about the project from start to finish. I told them I would be happy to but that the project was not my idea. It was someone else's, and I had no idea whatsoever how he dreamed it up, and that it certainly would not have occurred to me in a thousand years.

"When they asked me who this person was I told them, and they want you to come with me and speak to Congress. I don't know how you feel about that, but if we can get them to see this as a practical solution to the problems of our big cities, it could be a wonderful contribution to our country. I did not make a commitment but told the senator I would ask you, then get back to him."

For the first time since Daniel met Joshua, he seemed nervous and unsure of himself, not knowing how Joshua would react.

"My friend, I think it is a great idea. When do we go?"

"Joshua, I'll never understand you. I thought for sure you would be annoyed at having to make a public appearance when you are always so reticent. You would not even let us dedicate a building to you."

"This is different, Daniel. I've wanted to speak to those people for the longest time. I can't wait to tell them what's on my mind."

"They have to set the date," Daniel told him. "It may be a month or six weeks. We'll have plenty of time to prepare. Can you come over to the house tonight so we can spend more time talking about it?"

"I'd love to. I could use a good meal."

"Your friend Andrew knows you're here and was hoping you'd stop by his office to show you the details of the interior of the synagogue and the mosque."

"Good. I'll see you at dinner," Joshua said as he left Daniel's office.

Andrew was happy to see Joshua, and stood up as he entered the room.

"Joshua, please be seated. I'm so glad you stopped by. I've just completed the interior of the synagogue and the mosque, and wanted to show them to you."

Joshua walked to the drawing board and Timothy took out the architect's rendering of the interiors of the two buildings, showing them one done by computer in three dimensions. Joshua was impressed. The details were exquisite. Special artists had been imported from Israel and Saudi Arabia to design decorations in a way that would be sensitive to the religious traditions of the two congregations.

"Joshua, I am so happy you like them. It is my way of saying thank you for all the help you gave me when I was hurting."

"Andrew, you don't have to thank me. You are a good person, and all of us need help at times. We help one another. What you have done is a remarkable work of art. It is truly inspired. I am sure the people in both the congregations will be most pleased."

"If you are pleased, Joshua, that is all I am concerned about. That means a lot to me. You are my dearest friend."

"Thank you, Andrew. You have a great career ahead of you. Enjoy it."

The rest of the day Joshua spent at the new cultural center, watching the young people at their dancing lessons and art classes, and learning to play musical instruments. Jana was there as usual, in her glory seeing the children's enthusiasm. She showed Joshua around the building and explained all her dreams for the place. Later in the afternoon they went home for supper, so Daniel and Joshua could talk about their meeting with Congress.

The Spanish festival was a fun-filled affair. Joshua appeared as he had promised. The whole street was closed off. They had a big procession, with the band blaring its rousing hymns through the whole neighborhood. It was a happy celebration in honor of Jesus' Mother. As they paraded down the street, the people carried a life-size painting of Mary carrying Jesus in her arms. The preacher delivered a moving sermon, praising Mary as the perfect example of what a Christian should be, totally centering her life around Jesus. "If only we could imitate her in that. Living only for Jesus, she was the perfect follower of Jesus."

Joshua stood and listened. It brought back so many tender memories of his childhood. Tears welled up in his eyes, remembering how his Mother used to worry so much about him, ever conscious of Simeon's prophecy that her son "was destined for the rise and fall of many in Israel, and that her own soul a sword would pierce." Jesus' Mother had suffered so much over all that had happened to her Son. "She understands our mothers today who worry day and night about their children in this frightening, troubled city in which we live."

After the religious part of the service, the people celebrated till late at night, with music and dancing and Spanish foods of every type. Carmen spotted Joshua and ran over to him. She was dressed in an exciting, colorful Spanish costume. She was the center of attraction for the affair. Everyone was waiting for Carmen to dance. She was glad Joshua had arrived on time, so she could seat him right where she wanted him, in front.

When the time came for her to dance, all the noise stopped. She danced for over an hour, which would have exhausted almost anyone else, but she was just beginning to have fun. All during the dances she looked at Joshua, and at one point went over to him and went down on one knee and bowed before him, then took him by the hand and led a very reluctant man out in the middle of the crowd to dance with her. To her surprise, and everyone else's, after a few awkward steps he began to dance as smoothly and precisely as any professional. And he really enjoyed it, remarking to Carmen in the middle of the dance that he hadn't danced like this since he danced at a wedding party a long, long time ago. He had forgotten how much fun it was.

After a couple of dances, he sat down to everyone's applause as Carmen continued to dance with others.

When the celebration was over, Carmen ran over to Joshua and thanked him for coming, saying how much it meant to her. She had told everyone in the community all about the wonderful work he was doing and how he had touched so many lives.

Then, finally, she said to him, "Joshua, may I come and work with you? I would love to work by your side, bringing Jesus' love to the world. I saw what you did for Elijah and how you changed his life. I would consider it a great honor to be able to work with you."

"But I may not be here long," Joshua told her.

"Then I will carry on after you. The message and the work must continue."

"Well, if you really want to, but it won't be easy."

"I know, but I am strong and I can take a lot. It is not easy living where I live. I hope someday you can come and visit with my people here. They need you also."

"Carmen, I can see why Elijah loved you so much. You have a soul as clear as a pane of glass. Light and warmth shine right through you. Yes, come and work with me if you like. You will bring a happy spirit to the people, and perhaps revive some of the playfulness of Elijah."

"Thank you so much, Joshua. I love you," she said as she ran off into the crowd that was breaking up to go home.

XVIII

Time went by fast now that the development was finished. Life became so exciting for everyone, there were not enough hours in the day to enjoy it all. Georgeanne and her "family" moved into one of the new houses, not too far, it turned out, from Josephine and her family, and they fast became friends. The atmosphere created by the development was that of an old-fashioned neighborhood with a warm friendly feeling. The antique-style street lights added to the charm. People from the neighborhood trained to do landscaping planted the trees that lined the streets.

A strange thing, however, was taking place beneath the surface of the apparently serene appearances of the neighborhood. Daniel contacted Joshua late one morning and asked him to meet with him that night. It was urgent. They had not seen each other for well over a month and Daniel had some disturbing news to tell him.

Joshua went over to his house, and Daniel couldn't wait to tell him what had transpired since they last talked.

"The senator called this morning very upset. It had been agreed that the committee handling matters on urban development would sponsor the talk. No problem. The committee agreed on the date and invited all their colleagues in both houses to attend. No problem. Because of the widespread interest in the project and its implications for the rest of the country, the committee was sure the whole Congress would attend. Good.

"But then the oddest thing happened. Someone filed a

petition demanding Congress withdraw the invitation for you to speak to Congress on the ground that it was a violation of the separation of church and state. Can you imagine anything so ridiculous? The person filing the petition was a man named Lucius Fabian, and he contended that you were Jesus Christ, the Son of God, and God was forbidden by the Constitution to speak to Congress.

"Needless to say, Senator Moynihan was furious, as were all his colleagues. They immediately sensed a most uncomfortable predicament. The lawsuit would receive national attention. The interest of the whole country would be aroused. Everyone would be curious as to how their own senators and representatives would react: like wimps and back out of it, or fight the lawsuit and allow the talk to take place.

"Besides that, everyone would be curious as to the identity of this impersonator of Jesus Christ. So now, good friend," Daniel said in concluding, "what do you have to say to all this?"

"It should be interesting."

"That's all?"

"What would you like me to say?"

"Well, for starters, do they have a case?"

Joshua laughed with a deep belly laugh and was clearly having fun. "Daniel, Daniel, you are a foxy one! How should I know?"

"You're the only one who does know. That's why you're laughing. The senator is coming home tomorrow and wants to talk to you. You know what he is going to ask you. What are you going to tell him?"

"If I say I am Jesus Christ, then what? There are a lot of people locked up because they claimed to be Jesus Christ. If

I say I am not Jesus Christ, then that would seem to solve the problem."

"Would you be willing to swear to that under oath?"

"Why does it always have to come down to an oath? They really get mileage out of that oath."

Joshua still laughed though he knew he was trapped. Daniel also knew Joshua was trapped, and would give anything to know how Joshua would extricate himself.

"Joshua, do you have any idea who might be behind this?" Daniel asked him.

Joshua was silent for a long moment, then looked at Daniel. "Yes, I know well who is behind it. He is angry because I humiliated him before his followers. The steps we take to counter this must be done in silence. Satan has long ears, Daniel, and we must be careful not to show our hand. I know his every move, but he does not know mine, unless I choose to reveal them.

"We will meet with the senator tomorrow, and discuss the matter, and advise him what he should do. We will move one step at a time, never revealing the next move. Satan is arrogant and is inclined to overreach himself. If I do not reveal my moves beforehand, then I can count on him to miscalculate."

"Joshua, aren't you being melodramatic in blaming it on Satan?" Daniel asked.

"Most of the time it is not Satan who is behind evil happenings. People's selfishness and twisted minds inspire most of the evil we see around us. But this time I know it is Satan. Let it go at that, Daniel."

The next day Senator Moynihan arrived in the city and was met at the airport by Daniel and Joshua.

"Senator, this is Joshua. Joshua, Senator Moynihan,"

Daniel said, introducing the two men as they met at the gate in the terminal. They shook hands, exchanged pleasantries, then drove to a nearby restaurant and spent the next three hours discussing their concerns.

"Senator, I already explained to Joshua what you had told me over the phone yesterday morning. So he's up to date," Daniel said.

"Good. Joshua, do you have any idea who is behind this ridiculous lawsuit?" the senator asked him. "He obviously knows you, or thinks he does."

"Yes, his name is Lucius Fabian," Joshua replied. "He is possessed by an evil spirit, and recently led a community of Satan worshipers."

"Oh, young man, come off it. Don't try to feed me that kind of stuff," the senator said almost contemptuously.

"You asked me a question. I gave you my answer. If you don't believe me you are all going to make fools out of yourselves over this lawsuit," Joshua retorted matter-of-factly.

"What do you mean?" the senator asked him.

"A person I know belonged to the group and I was asked to save him. We went to the place of their worship one Sunday morning. When I walked in unexpectedly, the whole assembly panicked and the evil spirits left them. All except Fabian. He clung to his evil spirit and together they have sworn revenge. They think this is the way they will get it."

"How can you know this for a certainty?" the senator pressed.

"I watch their every move. Senator, when you have a colleague in Congress who opposes you, are you not keenly aware of every move he makes to outsmart you? If you are not, you had better be. In the same way I know each of

Satan's moves before he even makes them. So there is really no need for us to be overly concerned. He has already made his first move, a crude one for a being so superior. What do you think, Senator, does the lawsuit have any merit?"

"I talked to our lawyers and they seem to think it is a shrewd move, although they could not understand the motive behind it. To them it made no sense, accusing someone of being Jesus Christ as an argument for denying the person the right to speak to Congress. It seems ludicrous."

"On the surface, it does seem ridiculous until you understand their intention. This is why it is important for us to know what we are up against. The real battle is being fought beneath the surface of the mere lawsuit. Their intention is to force all of us into the national spotlight and try to embarrass us by trapping me into answering a question that is driving them insane."

"What question is that?" Daniel asked.

"My identity."

"If the Court decides that Jesus Christ can speak to Congress, then their plot is foiled, but they are too clever for that. They know the decision beforehand, and that it will be in their favor."

"Clever, Joshua. Our lawyers said the same thing. A recent case in Michigan is parallel to it. The Court ruled that a picture of Jesus could not be displayed in a school. If a picture of him cannot be displayed, a fortiori, He Himself in person would surely be banned."

"See, the strategy is shrewd. The next step will be to ask me to identify myself. I could either say I am just what you see, Joshua, or I could say I am Jesus, the Son of God. If I say I am Jesus, then I am either who I say I am, or I am

217

psychologically disturbed, which many throughout the country would think, perhaps even some of your colleagues, thereby discrediting me, or I could be asked to prove that I am Jesus. As I have no need to prove who I am to anyone, that request would go unheeded, and I would still be suspect. Satan is shrewd."

"Who are you, Joshua?" Senator Moynihan asked him point-blank.

"I am what you see. We have to be cautious. Satan cannot read my thoughts, but he can hear us speak. One step at a time. Let the lawsuit go through. Then we will make our next move, if you are still interested."

"More than ever. In fact, we really have no choice. The lawsuit will be national news. For us to back out of it now would make us look like real wimps, afraid of taking sides in a lawsuit banning God from Congress. Imagine how that would sit with our people back home!"

"I told you Satan is sly. Every move he makes is fraught with traps. If you make one move you are trapped, if you make the opposite move you are trapped. That is the way he works. Only an angel by your side can help you outsmart him. That is why we have to be wary. Talking about our next move will betray our hand. He has big ears. When the time comes we can make our next move."

"I have to admit, Joshua, even though I don't even know who you are, this looks like it is going to be a real adventure if you actually do know what you are talking about."

"Trust him, Senator," Daniel said. "He may look simple and naive, but I have found him to possess a mind more complex than any I have ever experienced. I stay awake nights analyzing simple statements he makes on occasions, statements revealing knowledge a human mind could not possibly acquire on its own."

"Well, this meeting certainly has been an eyeopener," the senator said. "I have to be home by supper, so I'll leave you gentlemen. I appreciate your coming here to meet me. I'll contact you as soon as I learn something more. It was a pleasure meeting you, Joshua."

"A pleasure meeting you, Senator."

"Daniel."

"Senator."

The three men parted, Daniel driving Joshua back to the city and to his house, where Joshua spent the evening. That night when he went to bed Daniel took a long look at the icon Joshua had given him and Jana. The more he stared at it, the more he wondered. He shared his thoughts with Jana.

"Dan," Jana said to him as they lay in bed, "I spent the whole day yesterday staring at that icon. That face. Joshua said it was a perfect representation of his mother. I got goose pimples over the thoughts going through my mind. Do you think?"

"I don't know, dear, but I can't help but feel we are in the presence of something, someone, very sacred. It is awesome. You know, Jana, when I look out the window of one of my offices overlooking the project, I can't believe the vast dimensions of the thing. My men could not have conceived anything so immense in a thousand years. I don't know of a developer who could even begin to imagine an undertaking so massive, and to think that Joshua just dreamed it up on the spur of the moment in response to a question I asked him that first evening. Uncanny!"

"Dear, how did your meeting go with the senator?"

"It went well, although I think Joshua mystified him. I think Senator Moynihan is confused after meeting him. Doesn't know whether he's a kook or a genius. I tried to assure him that he could feel comfortable believing whatever Joshua tells him, even if it sounds far-fetched. I think I convinced him. We'll see. Good night, Jana."

"Good night, dear."

XIX

NOW THAT SO many of Joshua's friends lived closer together in their neighborhood city, it was difficult for him to visit individual families. So they had to work together and plan for his visits. Either Josephine would invite Georgeanne and her "family" over to their house, or vice versa, or they would all meet in one of the little parks and have a picnic, and ask Joshua to talk to them, which he was only too happy to do. He was always a source of peace and comfort. Carmen came to the neighborhood almost every other day, sometimes after work, sometimes on her days off. She was fun to be with and radiated joy and a carefree Jesus spirit, which seemed to take away everyone's heartache for a while. They looked forward to her coming. Sometimes she would sing. Sometimes she would dance. She did not have to speak or give talks, her person radiated messages more expressive than a thousand talks, all subtle, all gentle, all with the same simple message: "Be happy, Jesus loves you and He is always by your side. You are never alone."

Whenever she came she always sat as close to Joshua as she could. Everyone smiled. They knew how much she loved him. They did too, but they never got jealous. Carmen was different. She was almost like a part of him, like his female other half, the two were so much alike. Joshua met with Carmen often, and shared many things with her, his thoughts, his dreams, his vision of things, how he felt about everything. As time went on, she seemed to mirror him in almost everything, but it was not put on. It was just that she loved him and could identify with him so easily, and personality-wise she was very much like him.

When Joshua could not be present, Carmen's presence would remind people of him. After a while, when she spoke it was almost like hearing Joshua, so much had she absorbed his spirit. Her happiness and spontaneous laughter made Josephine feel that Elijah was also present in her, and that brought her comfort.

Daniel contacted Joshua not long after their meeting with the senator to tell him the lawsuit had been heard and the judge ruled that, if Joshua was truly whom the plaintiff claimed he was, he could not be allowed to speak to Congress. It was important for the senator and Joshua and Daniel to have another meeting. The congresspersons decided that, since they had no reason to believe that Joshua was anything more than they accepted him to be, they would go ahead with his talk on the date already scheduled.

No sooner had they made the decision than Fabian and his cronies filed and received an injunction ordering the Congress not to schedule the talk until it could be determined what was the true identity of Joshua. It seemed ridiculous to the senator and his colleagues for the Court to rule that Christ could not speak to Congress, whatever the identity of Joshua might be. They appealed the matter to the Supreme Court.

The decision was returned in record time. According to the Constitution of the United States, it could not be legally justified for Jesus Christ to be invited to speak in Congress to the elected members of Congress, as His presence and the force of His person could have undue and unjustified influence over the decision-making responsibilities of officials elected to frame the laws of the country. If this man

Joshua was whom the plaintiffs claimed him to be, then it was illegal and unconstitutional for Congress, as representatives of the government and of the people, to invite and allow him to speak to them.

So Daniel and Joshua had to meet again with the senator at the airport. This time he brought other congresspersons and congressional lawyers as well. The meeting lasted for at least three hours. The heart of the issue was Joshua's true identity.

"Joshua," Senator Moynihan asked him with exasperation in his voice, "are you whom these people claim you to be?"

"Why is that important?" Joshua asked him.

"Joshua, you don't seem to understand. The issue is no longer you speaking to us. The issue is now something much deeper and, in all honesty, involves the reputations and political future of each one of us in Congress. If we give in to the Supreme Court decision, it will be interpreted by our people back home to mean that we went along with a decision forbidding God to speak to Congress. Can you imagine what our conservative constituents would do with that? We might as well quit right now. We'd all be recalled."

Joshua laughed, which annoyed them.

"You laugh," a lady senator named Allenby said.

"Yes, because you are taking this whole thing too seriously. This is a game, and it can be fun if you don't let yourselves get caught up in it."

"What do you mean, a game?" Senator Allenby pursued.

"I explained to Senator Moynihan at our last meeting what I meant. He can explain it to you on the way back to Washington. Our opponents are very disturbed about events they find threatening and have made a move to counter them. You countered with your move. They seem, to appearances, to have won. They did win a decision. But that is not the end of the game. The next move is yours. That is what we should discuss, the next move. My identity is irrelevant."

"All right, what then do you think should be the next move?" one of the lawyers asked.

"First of all, you have to remember, we are not fighting a simple battle on the level that appears on the surface. It is not just an attempt to annoy us by obstructing a talk. It is an attempt to force a showdown as a response to their panic."

"Who are the *they* you're talking about?" a senator asked with obvious irritation in his voice.

"The ones who filed the lawsuit. I happen to know them and what they stand for."

"What are you talking about, their panic, panic over what?" another congressman asked, also annoyed over what to him sounded like the raving of a person afflicted with paranoia.

"We are in the midst of a dreadful but unseen war. Until now powerful forces have been at work in this country and throughout the world to divorce God from His creation on the grounds that His influence is illegal and an unwanted intrusion on people's privacy. These forces have so far, by clever strategy, managed to neutralize God's influence over legislation throughout the country. There are no more absolute values determining morality. No more divine law. No longer any objective bases for the formulation of laws or court decisions. People who observe the divine law can find themselves in violation of civil law and can now be arrested and imprisoned, or penalized in other ways. With God gone, morality can now be determined by polls or by the wishes of the people. Rights can no longer be considered as coming from God. That consideration is no longer justifiable constitutionally. Rights are given by the government, expressing the wishes of the people, or the whims of an ever changing Supreme Court. The right to life no longer comes from God. It comes from a decision of the Court, which means that that right can be modified or abrogated whenever the Court deems it justifiable. The very institutions upon which civilization has rested for thousands of years are now called into question as unworkable and unjustifiable restraints on the arbitrary fads of the discontented.

"With this universal breakdown of the moral structure of the community, who then decides what is moral and what is not moral? A whole new moral code has to be formulated, as previous elements of the moral code influenced by the divine law are now considered irrelevant, illegal, and unconstitutional. Life and death are arbitrary values. Personal possessions and private ownership are rights granted by the Court, no longer inalienable rights coming from God. What will be the basis for this new moral code? What will be the source of people's no longer inalienable rights? God forbid that the time should come when the quality of a person's life should be judged by others to be of no real worth, or to be an unjustifiable inconvenience or embarrassment to those responsible for the person. That person's life then will hang merely on a court decision.

"Until now our opponents have had a wide-open field as they went about poisoning people's minds with only token opposition. But now they are frightened at what they see. They are frightened at the possibility that the Son of God, in the guise of a simple homeless man, may be allowed to speak to the highest decision-making body in the country, thereby exerting His powerful influence over their governing of the country. To them, it is the first dramatic manifestation of God's concern over what is happening to His creation, and in panic they must frustrate Him at every turn."

The group sat listening to Joshua spellbound. Whether he was right or wrong, whether he was just another paranoid seeing evil conspiracy behind every movement in society or the Son of God as the opponents believed, what he said made sense, particularly in light of what had been happening throughout the country, and they could not help but be impressed, and not a little frightened.

"If that is what is on our opponents' minds, the logical question then is, 'Are they right in making the assumption as to your identity?' " Senator Moynihan said, looking straight into Joshua's eyes.

"Whether they are right or not makes no difference. What is important is our next move," Joshua replied, again avoiding the question.

"What *do* you think should be our next move?" Senator Allenby asked, still not feeling comfortable about asking advice from a person who seemed to have little or no education and was nothing more than a homeless person with, perhaps, a big ego, concocting this conspiracy idea to make himself appear important. Why this wealthy, worldly billionaire sitting next to him was so enamored of him was beyond her comprehension.

"The next step should be to sidestep the decision of the Court. If you really would like Daniel and myself to speak to you and your colleagues, that can be accomplished in many ways. You do not have to do it as members of Congress. You can arrange the interviews as private citizens and hold the meeting outside the halls of Congress. There is no law against that. And as long as there is no use of public funds, no one can find that arrangement unconstitutional."

That seemed simple enough. No one could find any objection to that, so, feeling they had resolved the problem to everyone's satisfaction, their meeting broke up.

"Joshua, just one more question. Who are you, really? Can you tell us just to satisfy our own curiosity?" Senator Moynihan asked one last time.

Joshua laughed. "Ask Daniel," was all he said.

As they were walking out, some of the others who had not been too vocal at the meeting surrounded Joshua to ask him questions. Senator Moynihan pumped Daniel for his opinion as to Joshua's identity.

"You know, I am just as mystified as all of you. All I can say is the man has a mind so breathtaking in its scope, it is awesome. But, not too long ago, he gave me and my wife a present. It was an icon. He said it was a perfect likeness of his mother. As it was a painting of the Madonna, I merely thought he was telling me his mother looked like that. But, as Jana and I were examining the painting last night, the strangest thought struck both of us. Putting my hands over the veil surrounding the face, we just analyzed the features. They looked exactly like Joshua. If Jesus had no earthly father, all the genes would have come from his mother, and he would have looked just like her. Then I realized what he was telling me in his own cryptic fashion. Though we will never know for sure, will we? Senator, draw your own conclusions. I think I now have mine, and I feel blessed. I am dying to hear what he has to say to Congress."

"If that be the case, I can't wait either. It should be awesome. We will have to record it, at our own expense of course."

As the group returned to the airline terminal, Daniel drove Joshua home for supper. They had a delightful evening. Daniel was lighthearted and exuberant. Jana and Charlene were happy to be able to see Joshua for yet another evening. The night went by fast.

XX

THE DAY FOR the dedication of the whole development arrived. It was held in the park where a section was landscaped in the form of an amphitheater, so plays and concerts could be held in the open air. There were representatives from the White House, and the Congress, and political leaders from nearby and far away. The amphitheater was packed. When everyone was seated on the grass, the dignitaries processed in, Joshua walking in with Daniel and Jana and Charlene. In front of them were the mayor, the senators and representatives, and other high officials. As they walked through the aisle, security guards made sure the aisle was clear. Processing along with the others, Daniel and Joshua walked past a guard standing nearby. He looked at Joshua and immediately recognized him as the man he had driven out of the park that night, calling him a bum. The man turned beet red. Joshua looked at him and merely smiled kindly.

When everyone was on the stage, the ceremony began. "The Star-Spangled Banner" led the program, followed by a minister's prayer. Every dignitary present had to have his or her two minutes to say something profound. At the end the mayor gave a moving address and praised the generosity and genius of Daniel and Jana Trumbull for what was perhaps the greatest construction undertaking in the history of the world, considering that it was all done at one time. The mayor then introduced Daniel.

He did not speak very long, and in his humility, he said

he did not want to take credit for what everyone could see spread out before them and all around them. This project, he said, was his way of saying thank you to a man who did him and his wife a kindness for which they could never possibly repay him. "This development, as wonderful and breathtaking as it is, was the dream of a man whom the whole neighborhood knows. But they do not know him as an architect or a builder. They do not know him as a genius or as a man of high social standing, or even as a man of means. But he *is* an architect far beyond the reach of any I have ever known, and I have always, as you know, hired the best. And he *is* a builder par excellence, not a builder of buildings, but a builder of lives. His mind far exceeds our definition of genius. He has a mind that surpasses anything I have ever known. As for social standing, he feels most comfortable with the poor whose overlooked genius he understands and whose dignity he truly appreciates. It was they, by his insistence, who built this magnificent development, and who now operate it and everything in it. A man of means. Oh, if I could only lay bare my soul and tell you what I really know in my heart. What flows from that man's heart enriches the whole world. And yet he has walked among us as one who is poor, homeless, shunned by some as of no worth, a man who on many nights had no place to lay his head (though we would have gladly welcomed him), a man who never had a penny in his pocket, who wore clothes most of us would be ashamed to wear, a man who apparently had nothing, but who enriched the lives of so many, a man whom we in the neighborhood all know and have come to love. He is the one who, in answer to a simple question I asked him one evening, dreamed up this magnificent, awesome development on the spur of the moment. His simple dream, with all the details that flowed so effortlessly from that divine mind of his, took my three hundred architects and four hundred engineers all these many months to record and translate on paper. Joshua, please step forward so we can all thank you."

Shy, and more than a little embarrassed at having been exposed, he approached the microphone. The crowd stood and applauded for almost ten minutes. Though everyone knew and loved him, no one had ever dreamed that the project was his brainchild. He always appeared so humble and unassuming, and so simple.

When the applause finally stopped, a silence fell over the park. It was so quiet you could hear the birds singing. Joshua merely said to the crowd, "Rarely have I come across a couple so open to God as Daniel and Jana. It is their goodness and generosity that have made all this possible. But as magnificent as this awesome place is, it is nothing compared to the beauty of the home my Father has prepared for you. He is the only one worthy of the dedication of your lives. Love Him and serve Him in one another and love one another as I have loved you. Thank you all for your friendship and for your kindness to me."

He sat down. The applause was thunderous.

After that official dedication of the finished development, a string of individual dedications took place throughout the neighborhood, including the dedication of the new synagogue and the mosque. Joshua attended both of them. Before he arrived the religious leaders of both communities had found out they both owed the existence of such beautiful places of worship to Joshua. Joshua arrived at the dedication ceremonies as unobtrusively as possible so as not to be noticed, which is precisely what happened. When his name was mentioned during the dedication address, and he was asked to stand and come forward to say a few words, he was embarrassed. He always believed in not letting the left hand know what the right hand was doing, so would have preferred to stay anonymous.

He did, however, approach the microphone and say a few words in Hebrew at the synagogue, and in Arabic at the mosque. The gist of what he said was, "My friends, I am overjoyed to be here to celebrate with you these beautiful houses built to honor my Father and your Father. He is the same God, though we call Him by different names. Be open to His grace so you will see more clearly where He is leading you. I pray that as you worship here you will be mindful that you are not isolated strangers surrounded by a community of strangers. You are members of God's family, surrounded by other members of His family. Everyone around you are brothers and sisters. How you respond to them is how you respond to God, as they also are precious children of our Father. Do not isolate yourselves and restrict your love only to your own. It is not God's way. The sincerity of your love of God is manifest in how you express your love and care for others. God's love is not exclusive or restricted. He loves and reaches out to everyone. So must you. Love one another as God loves you."

It was short. It was simple. It was touching.

It was not long after their last meeting at the airport that Senator Moynihan called Daniel to tell him the talk was still on. However, the full Congress would meet outside the Capitol building and he and Joshua could speak to them on the steps of the Capitol. The sound system was being paid for by contributions from members of both houses. The senator told Daniel he would be honored if he and Joshua could come down the night before and stay at their house.

Daniel and Joshua took a flight for Washington the day before the talk. It was not a long flight. Daniel was too discreet to ask Joshua what he intended to wear. His clothes, always washed and pressed, were always the same.

Daniel was a good supporter of the senator, so this was a chance for the senator to show his gratitude. They had a marvelous evening. Joshua enjoyed himself and the conversation was light. When he was relaxed and not under pressure to say something world-shaking he was a lot of fun and had a fabulous sense of humor. He was at his best that night, which gave Senator Moynihan and his family a chance to see an entirely different facet of Joshua's complex personality.

The next day the talk took place. Senator Moynihan made a few formal introductions of important people present, then introduced Daniel, who gave a description of the development from start to finish, suggesting it could be used as a model for other places throughout the country. When he finished, the senator asked Daniel to introduce Joshua. Then Joshua rose, stood before the microphone, and began to speak.

"Honorable members of Congress, friends: I cannot tell you how long I have been looking forward to this moment. I respect you. You have been called to lead a people who have been chosen, chosen to be a beacon to a world that has been plunged into darkness, confusion, and violence. You live in an age when moral values that have been the foundation of civilization for thousands of years are being questioned and rejected as obstacles to personal freedom by individuals and groups who demand that their own untested version of morality be accepted by society. For them the divine law which had been the established foundation of the Constitution is considered irrelevant and an unlawful restriction of people's freedom. Indeed, the Creator Himself has been judged irrelevant to the public life of the people, and reference to His presence and His influence over the community is held to be unconstitutional, and should never be a consideration in the framing of laws or standards of moral behavior. Yet the Constitution and the rights flowing from it were founded immutably upon the recognition of His existence. Indeed, it is only because of His existence that rights can be considered to be inalienable. Eliminating His existence renders all rights, even the most sacred right to life, subject to the arbitrary and capricious decrees of the Court, so impressively shrouded in solemnity. The very foundations of civilization itself are being shaken and, indeed, may crumble if an unstable morality is allowed to replace the solid values of the past, values that developed in people strong moral fiber and a steady vision of right and wrong.

"Your role as legislators is critical not just to the immediate material needs of your individual constituencies, but in providing moral leadership to the whole world, which is fast losing its vision of goodness and risks reverting to barbarism. The world must see your leadership as based upon strong noble principles and not dictated by unworthy political considerations, so the nations of the world can respect your people for the integrity of their lives and the nobility of their ideals.

"You have been called by your people to represent them and work for the betterment of their lives, and for the common good of the country, but you have also been called by your Creator to work for and maintain the highest moral standards, and, because of the power and prestige with which God has blessed this land, to establish lofty ideals for the conduct of international affairs that will set the course of civilized society for generations to come.

"The sacredness and nobility of the individual as a child of God must be the basis and focus of all your deliberations and of the laws you formulate, as every law, no matter how seemingly far removed, ultimately redounds to the good or the detriment of the individual.

"We have been invited to speak with you today about a housing and building development. They are only stones and wood and dirt. It is the meaning and the purpose that inspired the development that is important. I just explained to you briefly the values that underlay that building project: the sacredness of the individual, and respect for the dignity of people whatever their temporary social or economic condition. That development will succeed because it recognizes people's innate desire to achieve and to better themselves and their families. It is not just a jungle of cages stacked high one upon another as a way of getting people off the streets, with no consideration for all their other legitimate needs.

"The development will go far in pointing to a solution to the problems facing the poor throughout the country and the world. You cannot just build houses. You must build communities, communities where work and play are integrated into the lives of the people.

"You may wince at the cost. The cost is insignificant if you consider it an investment in the future. The cost for all the failed projects of the past is staggering, especially since they are now recognized as a failure which makes their cost unjustifiable when the original problem still exists.

"But the project itself is just a project. It is the people who are important, and it is their needs that are important. You cannot just house and feed them. You do that for animals. It is the role of government to build the environment, with the help of industry, in which people can, without insurmountable difficulty, find the means to fulfill their dreams and satisfy their legitimate aspirations.

"Ladies and gentlemen, your calling is a noble one. It is your responsibility to preserve for future generations the rich heritage you have received. You must maintain your ideals, be strong in character, and have a firm understanding of what is important for the common good of the whole people and not just what is demanded to satisfy the inconvenience of the few. You must be like a beacon over rocky shores, providing stability and security in the darkness, and like the guidance system on a rocket that stays unerringly on course, not like a weather vane that changes with every shifting wind, thereby becoming useless yourselves and your noble calling merely a self-serving job with ever questionable benefits.

"You are captains of the ship guiding the civilization. Steer it wisely, prudently, selflessly until it reaches its port of call, the eternal kingdom where you will turn over your logbook and account for how you executed your watch and your guardianship of God's family."

The members of Congress sat all through the talk pondering deeply each word. When Joshua finished, they stood on the steps and applauded loudly and for a long time. Television cameras from all the networks and cable companies recorded the whole event for the evening news. Daniel congratulated him on the stirring talk he had given.

"I thought you might have been nervous about speaking in public, especially under these circumstances, but you seemed so calm and relaxed, like a real professional," Daniel said to Joshua when he finished speaking.

"Well, I have had a little experience at it, so I wasn't too anxious," Joshua replied jokingly.

Senator Moynihan and a few of the others surrounded Joshua and Daniel afterward, and barraged Joshua with questions, which he answered calmly and to the point. Everyone was impressed.

For a few hours afterward, Daniel showed Joshua around the city, then they left for home.

XXI

WALKING THROUGH THE resurrected neighborhood was a joy for Joshua. Seeing happy, smiling faces on people as they went to work in the morning, whistling and singing, made his coming worth while. So different from before, when there was no hope. Now practically everyone worked. Those who had marginal abilities kept the parks and the playgrounds and the streets immaculate and found a new sense of dignity when they could so graphically see the fruit of their labor and also how everyone appreciated their keeping the whole development so beautiful.

"It is so simple," Joshua reflected as he walked through a park one day, "when people really care and don't just use their vast resources to build up personal financial empires. Those are the kinds of people my Father has no room for in His kingdom, though most are highly respected in the kingdom on earth, because they lavishly honor its important people."

Joshua knew his work was coming to a close. This time it was with a certain sadness. He would have liked to stay and inspire others, but the real kingdom is not on earth. This is such a transitory and illusory existence, and so fragile. It should not be the object of people's dreams to live only for the building up of this kingdom, only to live here in dignity, but they should dream of the kingdom where real treasures lie, and where the happiness is endless, and the love and joy in God's presence far surpasses the most thrilling of any ecstasy we may experience in this kingdom on earth.

People looked for Joshua each day and were sad when they could no longer see him walking through the streets and the parks, and lightening the burdens of those who met him along the way, but they knew he was close though they could not see him, and as time went on they wondered, and began to realize that their lives had been graced and touched ever so gently by the presence of the very Love that created them, Emmanu-el.